THE SCIENCE OF SERVICE

(**MARK COLGATE,** Ph.D.)

+

THE

SCIENCE

—— OF ——

SERVICE

=

The **Proven Formula** to Drive **Customer Loyalty** and **Stand Out** from the Crowd

●● **PAGE TWO** BOOKS

ISBN 978-1-989025-06-2 (hardcover)
ISBN 978-1-989025-25-3 (ebook)

Produced by Page Two Books
www.pagetwobooks.com
Jacket design by Taysia Louie
Interior design by Taysia Louie
Interior photos by Mark Colgate

Printed and bound in Canada by Friesens

18 19 20 21   5 4 3 2 1

Distributed in Canada by Raincoast Books
Distributed in the US and internationally
by Publishers Group West

https://markcolgate.com/

Contents

This book is dedicated to my mum, who died shortly before I finished writing this book. Mums are magic; they cast a spell on us, an enchantment that always draws us to them. Once the spell was broken, I realized it was more powerful than I had ever imagined. Mum, your brand of magic is something I miss so much every day. Goodbye xxxxx

Introduction

Creating Famous Service

"**A**RE YOU READY for an amazing adventure?" shouted Winton, the driver of the Kiwi Experience bus, as it climbed to the top of an extinct volcano on a beautiful sunny morning in Auckland. It was the start of a trip around New Zealand for forty like-minded travellers who were unprepared for the driver's burst of enthusiasm as the panoramic view unveiled itself.

Virtually all of the travellers were unsure of what to expect from this trip, apart from what they had learned from the company's marketing materials. One of the passengers, Rory Gillies, a burly twenty-three-year-old Scotsman, had heard great things about Kiwi Experience while travelling around Australia. He was curious to find out what made this service experience so successful and so different from the others offered in New Zealand. Before boarding the bus, Rory had approached Winton.

"Have you been busy this summer?" Rory asked.

"It feels like I haven't stopped," said Winton. "I can only remember once or twice when my bus wasn't full."

"So, what makes Kiwi Experience so famous?" asked Rory.

"If I told you, it would ruin the experience," Winton said, "but jump on and maybe I'll give you a few ideas along the way."

Rory gave Winton the thumbs-up and he walked down the bus's aisle. He was travelling alone and felt a wave of loneliness as he sat next to another solo traveller. What Rory didn't know was that he wouldn't feel lonely again, not even for a minute, during the three weeks he spent on the Kiwi Experience.

Kiwi Experience has become famous for delivering an amazing service experience. Like Rory, I travelled on the Kiwi Experience (too many years ago for me to mention), and I later did market research for them for six years when I lived in New Zealand. As a passenger, a market researcher, and an interested observer of their continued success, I realize they provide a compelling starting place to understand how to deliver an exceptional customer experience. We'll be revisiting Kiwi Experience throughout the book as we determine how a company can break away from its competitors and build its service fame.

I've been studying service organizations and working with firms like Kiwi Experience for more than twenty years. This book is a summary of the science, systems, and discipline of great customer experiences. By the "science of service," I am referring to a well-established body of research that incorporates social and other branches of psychology, behavioural science, expertise theory, and even biology. Through findings from this research, as well as case studies from my own experiences improving companies' service, this book shows that delivering an excellent customer experience requires a lot of effort, innovation, practice, and patience—more than you ever imagined. Please don't be discouraged: if you can keep your focus when those around you are losing theirs, then you will deliver a consistently memorable customer experience, develop customer loyalty, and become famous for the best possible reasons.

Consistency is king, not the customer

You are probably wondering why I would write in a customer service book that the customer is not king, because they are ... aren't they? Sorry, don't take this personally. You are a very nice and extremely popular person, but, in this case, you are wrong.

Of course, customers are very important. But when you call the customer "king," you lower the importance of the employees delivering the service, which we simply can't do. As they say at the Ritz-Carlton, it's "ladies and gentlemen serving ladies and gentlemen." Both are equally important and you can raise the engagement levels of both by consistently delivering high-quality service. This is why consistency sits on the customer service throne.

In everything we do, we must seek consistency. As Jim Collins and Morten Hansen wrote in their book *Great by Choice*, "The signature of mediocrity is not an unwillingness to change. The signature of mediocrity is chronic inconsistency."[1]

A/B testing

In the workshops I facilitate for companies, I ask groups of participants—who range from executives to front-line staff—to share stories about companies they believe are *inconsistent* in delivering high levels of customer service—the naughty service providers, whom we avoid. After the lively discussion, I then have them talk about companies that are *consistent* in delivering high levels of customer service—the good or even great service providers.

Once we've finished these two steps, I ask a few people to share with everyone in the room what great customer service companies do well and what ill-disciplined companies do poorly. The stories are always fascinating and bring to life the topic of customer service. As you may have guessed already, this exercise is just a clever ruse, so I can sneak away for a thirty-minute massage and facial and come back fully rejuvenated and exfoliated.

I then have people vote on which experiences they most often have in their lives as consumers, or in the B2B context. They vote A if most are with companies that are consistent in delivering customer service or B if most are with companies that are inconsistent in delivering customer service.

I always use educational voting technology, such as iClicker or a polling app, to ensure that people are voting authentically. I have done this all over the world—in China, the U.S., New Zealand, Ireland, England, Canada, Bulgaria, Australia, the Philippines, and Guatemala—and, surprisingly, the results are consistent. About 15–20 percent of people vote A and the rest vote B. Put another way, for 80–85 percent of people voting, the majority of their experiences are with inconsistent service firms.

After the voting, we spend a little time unpacking why this may be the case. Participants often say that it's because we remember the bad experiences more than the good, and we end up telling eight or nine people about bad experiences and only one or two people about good experiences. That's actually one of the biggest customer service myths around. Overwhelming evidence tells us that word-of-mouth recommendations or condemnations are driven by entertainment.[2] We like telling entertaining stories, good or bad. Further, we often won't tell a negative customer experience story, even if it's entertaining, if we played a role in that negative experience and made ourselves look like idiots. "Mark, did you really think it was a good idea to bring an inflatable seat onboard the plane and refuse to move from business class?"

Ultimately, the workshop participants agree that firms that always provide high levels of customer service are simply very hard to find.

The challenge

So why haven't most organizations achieved service fame?

1. **Most organizations have not taken a scientific approach to service.** Organizations are often willing to take a scientific approach to budgeting, process excellence, and hiring, but the same is not the case for customer service. Virtually every organization would agree that customer service is important, but very few are willing to continually learn, invest, and experiment in the science behind it.

2. **Most organizations have not built a system for service excellence.** If there is no clear connection between the vision and strategic priorities of the company and customer experience, no measures in place to represent what great service means to the customer, no process for identifying and fixing customer pain points, and no method for linking employee rewards and recognition for achieving customer-focused goals, then companies are reinforcing the wrong types of behaviours.

3. **Most organizations underestimate the difficulty of consistently executing high levels of customer service.** Always providing customer service *that is appreciated by customers* is all about endurance. Think about running a marathon: you may have trained extensively and prepared carefully, but ultimately running the race is a test of persistence, resolve, and commitment. Even with a knowledge of the science of service, discipline is required to keep the customer service effort landing with every customer and in every interaction, especially when the going gets tough.

I took a three-year leave of absence from the University of Victoria, where I am a professor, to help the Commonwealth Bank of Australia improve its customer service. Commonwealth Bank is the tenth largest bank in the world, with twelve million customers and 40,000 employees. The Commonwealth Bank was the worst of the five major banks in customer satisfaction in Australia when I joined as general manager of that department in 2007. Since 2012, they have been the best bank in Australia which at the time of writing, was every year for five years. It took us longer than we had anticipated to achieve that goal, and that is a great lesson. It takes patience to get there and endurance to stay there, something the Commonwealth Bank has done.

By the end of this book, you will have the science, tools, and frameworks to create your own high level of consistent customer service. It's not fast or easy, but based on my work with companies that have achieved it, I can tell you that it's absolutely worth investing the time, effort, and money in ramping up the customer experience.

Of course, you could find the above sentence in any customer service book. Given that this book is based on the *science of service*, I will discuss the scientific reasons why organizations that prioritize customer service have higher financial returns[3,4] and more satisfied customers. You will learn how to use the science of customer service to build your organization's unique brand in the eyes of its customers. This brand includes how you serve your customers, how you innovate with customer service, and how your organization communicates its service brand to your customers in a compelling, clear, and memorable way.

While this book is focused on how organizations can build their reputations through great customer service, it is also about how *you* can build your personal brand and become famous for continually providing outstanding customer service. Most of the principles in this book apply on the individual level, as well as to organizations—how you treat your customers, how you win them over even when they're hard to deal with, how your own unique brand is reflected when you deliver service, and how you can stand out from the crowd. Every time you serve a customer—an internal customer (e.g., your colleagues) or an external customer (the "end" customers, who buy your service or product)—you either build your personal brand or diminish it.

Finally, on page 39, I'll ask you to explore science even further in a chemistry experiment where you sprinkle iron filings on top of a Bunsen burner. Okay, I made that last bit up, but don't you feel some chemistry between us already? Don't you think we could be great friends?

Science can be applied to improve a company's customer service, which in turn strengthens a community. For the last four years in Whistler—a world-renowned skiing town in Canada—we educated more than 16,000 people in the science of service and how to deliver outstanding customer service. Many people now travel to Whistler to receive the training. A whole town, including the company Whistler Blackcomb, with more than 4,300 employees, is delivering higher levels of customer service based on the approach outlined in this book.

The Commonwealth Bank and Whistler have become famous for their customer service by using the science behind it. So how do *you* develop your service brand?

Determine your own FAME

This scientifically driven approach to customer service can be understood with the FAME model. When you deliver on all four of its parts, you open yourself up to superior performance and long-term success.

F = Build a compelling *framework* by using the science of service.
A = Create *accountability* so everyone feels responsible for delivering great service.
M = Deliver *moments* of power.
E = Understand the key disciplines that create *endurance*, so you have a never-ending ability to grow your customer service levels.

This book uses case studies to show the FAME model in action. My work with the town of Whistler, in particular, highlights the key theme of the book: if you appreciate and execute the science of service and build a system around it, then increasingly higher levels of customer service and sales are inevitable. The Whistler case studies will surprise you and empower you to see customer service in a new way.

I've also included other random service stories throughout the book to keep you entertained, because reading a business book should not be like playing chess: utterly boring. I was playing chess with my son the other day and he said, "Dad, let's make this interesting." So we stopped playing chess.

But before we launch into the FAME model, let's consider: What is your goal? What are you aiming to achieve through customer experience? Your goal should always be to build a strong brand. Whether you are a for-profit, non-profit, government department, small organization, large organization, law firm, or cheese firm, you need to build an enduring brand—a brand that people love, will return to, and refer to others. Once you understand how to build a strong brand, then you can leverage service to increase its strength.

1

Building a Strong Service Brand

"**H**OW DID YOU enjoy Waitomo Caves?" Winton asked Rory at a stop en route to Rotorua.

"Amazing," Rory said. "I also really enjoyed the candlelit walk you took us all on through the Ruakuri Scenic Reserve to see the glow worms. Then a group of us from the coach went down to the Waitomo tavern for a few drinks—I feel a bit fragile today!"

Winton laughed. It seemed Rory was slowly understanding what the Kiwi Experience was all about.

The Kiwi Experience strives to be the best in the market for people who want to see the real New Zealand. Backpacking is all about travelling, meeting other people, getting value for money, and becoming involved in the local environment and culture. Kiwi Experience is an adventure transport network that allows backpackers, adventurers, and other like-minded travellers to choose where and on what they want to spend their limited travel funds. Kiwi Experience (KE) works on a high-volume, low-margin model where minimizing costs is key.

The fundamental concept behind the venture, formed in December 1988 by three partners, was to create a coach transport network that was neither an express point-to-point service nor an inflexible coach tour. Instead, KE set out to create a transport tour experience that had the advantages of both without the inherent drawbacks of either. It offers the flexibility of a traditional express service—in that customers get on or off the bus where they want—in addition to the guidance, information, and access to excitement-oriented places that a good adventure tour offers.

When the first bus set out in late 1989, this travel style was an innovation in the marketplace and the first of its kind in the world. In fact, the concept was so original that staff at KE initially had to spend much of their time explaining it to potential customers, clarifying that passengers could get on and off the coach wherever they liked—on a pass that lasted for six months—and still be part of an adventure trip that would take them to places off the beaten track. In fact, more than 90 percent of customers break their journey at some point, which proves that this concept is popular with KE's more than 400,000 travellers. Today, many copies of the KE concept can be seen all over the world.

Neil Geddes, one of the founders of the company, outlines the concept:

> I have always thought that a coach was a great way to get around, as meeting people is one of the fun things about travelling. But I could never understand the fact that everyone is stuck on one coach and you all had to do the same things. I don't believe you can create the ideal holiday for more than just the one person—this is why Kiwi Experience was invented.

Kiwi Experience has now grown beyond what the original owners ever thought possible and it's thanks to one factor—they determined their own FAME by designing a powerful experience, the heart of any strong brand.

When Geddes was asked what makes the Kiwi Experience so good, he had a simple reply.

> We ensure we give the customer what they want better than anyone else. Our service is not designed around what is good for the drivers;

it is designed around what is good for the customer. We are close to our market; we are proud to be close to our market. When we [the directors of Kiwi Experience] travel, we stay in backpackers' hostels, in order to learn and understand what the market wants. That is how we ensure that we always offer the best possible service for our clients. That is our core strength.

Because Kiwi Experience was the first in its marketplace, it took the lead in understanding what its target market wants and how it can service those needs effectively. The company's staff realizes that the backpackers' interactions with the coach's driver and with each other help create the "Kiwi Experience."

Another of KE's major appeals is the enormous number of paid excursions and activities they offer. From swimming with dolphins to skydiving, the list is almost endless. By purchasing a bus ticket, a passenger receives discounts on many activities throughout New Zealand. Kiwi Experience differentiates itself from its competitors with some exclusive activities and discounts.

What KE teaches us is that a brand must represent a *valuable market offer*, a concept that resonates with your target market and distinguishes you from the competition. Without this offer, there is really no brand at all.

Four dimensions of a strong brand

While there is much debate over the pragmatic value of most academic papers, service research guru Leonard Berry's "Cultivating Service Brand Equity" is, in my opinion, one of the most practical business papers ever written. Through his in-depth research with twelve firms, Berry ascertained that strong service brands have four main characteristics. (I have adapted the titles of these characteristics.)[1]

1. **Determine a valuable market offer.** Strong brands count for something that is important to the target customer—a prized market offer.

2. **Internalize the brand.** Employees who believe in the brand, because they understand the purpose of the company and are engaged at work every day, pass their passion on to the customer and help to create a strong brand for the company.

3. **Carve out a personality.** Strong service brands create a distinct, visible personality in the way they present themselves.

4. **Emotionally connect.** People prefer brands they can connect to emotionally, which creates a sense of trust and affection that is hard to imitate and harder to fake.

Let's look at each in turn with examples.

1. Determine a valuable market offer

This is the most important dimension, as the Kiwi Experience story highlights. If you don't create a market offer that distinguishes you from the competition and is valued by customers, then the other dimensions of a strong brand simply won't matter.

This book is littered, in a very nice way, with cases and examples of firms that created a unique service offer. Let's look at Salesforce, a cloud computing company based in San Francisco, California. Salesforce was the first company to develop customer relationship management (CRM) software that actually delivered upon its promised insights. Its CRM software is an enterprise solution that helps other companies manage tasks and relationships with new and existing customers.

Salesforce created a distinctive offer in four ways. First, it focused on offering a "software as a service" solution (a licensing model in which access to the software is provided on a subscription basis, with the software located on external rather than in-house servers) before anyone else. In fact, Salesforce coined this term, establishing themselves as the de facto leader in a new category of software.

Businesses can take advantage of Salesforce's cloud computing, with access to a complete set of cloud-based applications, a cloud platform, and a cloud infrastructure, making it cost effective. No need for software installations. Salesforce tightly defined software as a service in a way that made their approach unique. They centred their "no software" mantra (even in their logo) and hammered that message into the market consistently over many years.

Second, the flexibility gained through the cloud allowed companies complete freedom in implementing and using Salesforce's software. The CRM is 100 percent customizable and can be made to work in whatever fashion a business desires, which customers love. This customization has led to Salesforce beyond CRM to become a data-centric cloud platform upon which almost any business process can be modelled.

Third, Salesforce opened up its platform to developers to build custom applications and then provided an application directory, AppExchange, to promote and distribute them in a frictionless fashion. This single innovation continues to be one of the greatest competitive barriers to newcomers—hundreds of fully integrated applications complete the picture for mid-market and enterprise customers who would otherwise need to put that package together themselves.

Finally, Salesforce was very clever about how it evolved its pricing over time. It offered low-end software that minimized the barrier to adoption. It then had a per-seat subscription fee (since more users equals more revenue), with the price per subscriber increasing based on tiers of functionality. The result is geometric growth in revenue driven by its successful customers.[2]

Salesforce is a great example of a company making clear choices to create a distinctive offer and, in doing so, building a unique service brand.

2. Internalize the brand

Great brands are predicated on employees who believe in and are engaged with it. If the employee does not believe in the purpose of the brand, they're not excited about where it is going, and they don't personally connect with it, then they are unlikely to deliver a great experience for the customer.

You might think of Costco as a great instance of a brand that has created a valuable market offer with its membership cards, large warehouses stocked with extremely competitively priced products, and exceptional customer service. Take back a half-eaten cake to Costco, and they won't ask any questions before refunding you. But Costco builds its internal brand by paying its hourly workers an average of $20.89 an hour. By comparison, Walmart's average wage for full-time employees in the United States is $11.82 an hour.[3] Costco's CEO W. Craig Jelinek said, "We know it's a lot more profitable in the long term to minimize employee turnover and maximize employee productivity, commitment, and loyalty. If you treat consumers with respect and treat employees with respect, good things are going to happen to you."[4]

Costco is consistently rated as one of the best places to work and is frequently called the "happiest company in the world."[5] If you work hard to help employees believe in and trust the brand, then they will pass on that enthusiasm to customers (internal or external customers), be more productive, and stay longer with the company. The science of service shows that if you look after your employees, build their sense of purpose, and care for them, they will care for your customers.[6]

Building a strong brand inside a company means continually engaging employees on where the organization is going, sharing research on what customers think of the brand, showing how the company can do a better job in the customer's eyes, and coaching employees to deliver brand-building behaviours when they are in front of a customer.

3. Carve out a personality

Great service brands also carve out a distinct personality in the way they present themselves. IKEA has its distinctive logo and colours, its clever and fun advertising, and the unique experience within its stores. It has made some very funny TV commercials, one of which was voted one of the top ten most influential Canadian ads (Google "IKEA start the car.")[7] There is a very clear personality and image: playful, modern, and a little funky. What's interesting about IKEA is that it is obviously more famous for how it has a created valuable market offer in terms of clever product design, flat-packaging, and low prices.

To build a strong brand, you need to build awareness through distinctive logos, colours, advertising, social media, and sometimes humour, which can make a huge difference. Other noteworthy examples of companies carving out a personality are Telus, a telecom provider in Canada, with its use of loveable critters in its advertisements, and GEICO, with its adverts using much humour and even a talking gecko.

Think of your friends who have a distinctive personality; they stand out from the crowd and are memorable. It's likely you want to be with them more than others. The same goes for an organization. If it wants to stand out from the crowd and attract customers, it has to find distinctiveness and an edge to give it a unique personality.

4. Emotionally connect

Customers prefer brands that they have an emotional connection with, ones that create a sense of trust and affection. Think Disney. Disney represents our childhood, complete with compelling stories and a sense of adventure. Disney theme parks work hard to build the emotional connection between the visitors, employees, and Disney characters.

Many of you may be thinking, "Sure, it's Disney. It's easy for *them* to create an emotional connection." But every time the employee meets the customer, like in a Disney theme park, the employee and the firm have an incredible opportunity to build an emotional connection with the customer by personalizing the experience, having a great conversation, and giving the customer their undivided attention. Undoubtedly, it is easier for some organizations than others to create the emotional connection, but it is possible in every environment. We can even do this remotely, through chat rooms, emails, and call-centre staff. Amazon is one of the most trusted brands in the world and was recently voted the most trusted brand in the U.S.,[8] a great example of how an emotional connection can be built even in a virtual environment.

As Leonard Berry wrote, "Great brands always make an emotional connection with the intended audience. They reach beyond the purely rational and purely economic to spark feelings of closeness, affection, and trust. Consumers live in an emotional world; their emotions influence their decisions."[9]

I would like you to think about the emotional connection *you* build with your customers. Do you create a sense of affection, closeness, and trust in how you treat internal and external customers? How could you be more effective at building that emotional connection with your customers and the people that you serve inside the company? I'll discuss how to build an emotional connection in chapter 6.

CASE STUDY: T-Mobile—A revolutionary way to build a strong brand

A FANTASTIC EXAMPLE of a strong brand built using all four dimensions is T-Mobile, with its "Un-carrier" strategy. T-Mobile aims to be the exact opposite of the traditional telecommunication carriers in the United States—think contracts, rigid rules, and thick layers of bureaucracy. Prior to May 2013, when T-Mobile adopted this strategy, it had the lowest market share of the four major telecommunications companies, at 10 percent, and was lagging severely in terms of profitability. And its brand was weak in one key aspect—it had no offer that was considered unique and valuable in its target market's eyes.

However, since it chose this new approach, T-Mobile has grown from thirty-three million customers to seventy-three million customers. That growth has catapulted its market share from 10 percent to 18 percent, enabling it to surpass Sprint and become the number three U.S.-based operator.[10] In the process, it has built a strong brand.

Chief marketing officer Mike Sievert states that their plan in 2013 was to reimagine T-Mobile as the Un-carrier, the rebel small telecom that defies the rules written by its entrenched, bureaucracy-locked competitors. In short, it aimed to create a unique service offer.

Sievert states, "We don't think the consumer is best served by a mentality of an industry that has, for a long time, been dominated by utility companies that have utility company thinking." But where there are problems, there are opportunities. Sievert believes T-Mobile had "a real opportunity to be disrupters."[11]

The idea was to win back customers by changing the rules of the wireless carrier game. Smartphone subsidies disappeared, along with contracts. So did hard data caps and the expensive overages that kicked in when you accidentally went over your data limit. Any data left from the previous month rolled over. The message was clear to customers: pick any phone you want, use it as much as you want, quit whenever you want.

This branding approach began when the company introduced a streamlined plan for new customers that dropped overage fees for data and early termination fees. Many of the incumbent telecoms locked in customers to contracts they didn't want or profited from their mistakes (going over their data plan, for example), but T-Mobile's strategy was to introduce continual innovations to overcome these pain points.

There have since been twelve Un-carrier programs (such as no contracts, free international roaming, unlimited data). T-Mobile positioned itself as the challenger brand with products and services that its competitors were not willing to offer. It's a great message in any industry (think banking!). The problem is that most organizations are not brave enough to take this approach.

CEO John Legere states, "My number one job is to bring the Un-carrier to life—both for our customers and for our people." He continues, "Here at T-Mobile, that means making this a challenging, inclusive, and diverse workplace where we can all be ourselves and do what we do best—solve customers' pain points. And it means making sure our people share in this company's success by making them owners through annual stock grants."[12]

The evidence is that employees love this branding approach. For example, since 2013, T-Mobile has won sixty-two local and national "Best Places to Work" awards and accolades—almost all based on employee survey responses. And in a recent anonymous internal survey, 93 percent of T-Mobile employees said they take pride in working for T-Mobile.[13] The employees have internalized the brand; it's working for them and customers alike.

T-Mobile brought the Un-Carrier strategy to life through positioning, framing the discussion, and communications. It was supported by humorous advertising (advertising is easy when you have something to say!) in which an inept phone user welcomes the opportunity to get a new phone when needed. T-Mobile's JUMP! campaign was led by some outrageous (think Steve Jobs–style) presentations by John Legere talking about why customers are switching to T-Mobile.[14]

T-Mobile pitched the competition as exploitative and suggested they need to be defeated. John Legere continually said the competition was "greedy" and "they hate you [as customers]." Legere acknowledges he spoke from the heart (and often very close to the line) as a way to connect with his employees and customers. He sees himself and presents himself as a man of the people, not as a stiff executive. He continually stirs the pot by trash-talking the competition and getting in customers' faces when launching the Un-carrier offers. Watch, for example, "T-Mobile Presents Un-carrier Amped—Teaser Trailer" or "Pets Unleashed T-Mobile Un-commercial." Those ads say so much about T-Mobile—what they stand for and who you're choosing to be a customer of. The company has carved out a truly distinctive personality and has been able to emotionally connect with customers.

The T-Mobile disruption was driven by an understanding of basic customer frustrations and complaints. From inattentive customer service to complex bills and hidden fees, the pain points in the wireless industry were an open secret. While some consumers take on the telecommunications carriers, most decide to merely pay through the teeth and consider it a small sacrifice to obtain wireless service. T-Mobile tackled this head on to connect with its customers and potential customers. "T-Mobile fights for customers" could be a tagline for its approach.

T-Mobile went from weak and lagging (no unique offer, low employee loyalty, no distinctive personality, no connection with customers) to a very strong service brand within a few years, by maximizing the impact of all four dimensions of a strong brand. Its April 2018 share price is up 230 percent from April 2013 figures. Verizon's, Sprint's, and AT&T's have all remained static in that same timeframe.[15]

Strong financial returns and strong service brand equity are a great recipe for long-term success.

RANDOM STORY:
The Start of My Service Journey

AFTER I'D FINISHED my Ph.D. in Ireland, I had a dream of working in New Zealand or Australia. I'd travelled there when I took a gap year after university, which is when I went on the Kiwi Experience bus and started my journey of researching and understanding service excellence.

When I landed a job at the University of Auckland as a researcher and teacher, one of my colleagues at my current university said, "I went there once, but we couldn't get off the plane because New Zealand was shut."

Living in New Zealand for six years was not like living in Australia (see Random Story #1 in my first book). While Australia offers so many ways to die from scary stuff, New Zealand has not one scary thing. *None*. Many of the birds can't even fly at you. While I lived there, the scariest thing that made news was an infestation of tiger moths, which are harmless but—terrifyingly—coloured like tigers.

New Zealand is gentler and slower-paced but very forward-thinking, and it is certainly always open for business. In fact, it is more technologically progressive than most countries, being one of the first to adopt cellphones, texting, and internet banking. When I arrived in North America in 2002, I was amazed at how far ahead New Zealand was compared to the U.S. and Canada in terms of texting and electronic banking. (Cheques are still in use here in North America, but they have hardly been used in New Zealand since 2000.)

The Kiwis' obsession with technology caused me to implement what I thought was a very clever rule in my classrooms. In 1996, when cellphones really took off in New Zealand, students were very bad at turning them off and phones frequently rang during class. I created a rule that anyone whose phone went off would have to stand up and tell us their deepest, darkest secret. This worked for many years and then spectacularly backfired twice. You guessed it: *my* phone went off. To my embarrassment, I had to stand up and tell one of my deepest secrets—which I will not reveal to you now. Let's just say the students never quite had the same respect for me again!

I finally stopped using the rule when the students ganged up and played a fantastic prank on me. One of the students deliberately rang another in the middle of class. When her phone rang, I asked her to stand up and tell a secret. She said, "Mark, I am in love with you and now I have a chance to tell everyone in the class my feelings." The whole class burst into laughter as they saw my face turn pale. I've never used that rule since.

New Zealand is remote, whichever way you cut it. But don't let that put you off. New Zealand it is an incredible country to visit, and it really is a once-in-a-lifetime experience. Not like Australia, which is a once-in-a-lifetime experience because you're likely to die.

Recap

Creating a valuable market offer, and delivering a unique customer experience, is the starting point for building a strong brand; without this, your brand will never be distinct. Internalizing the brand then creates a passion you can pass to your external customers. Providing support and tools for your employees, so they emotionally connect with your customers, skilfully uses the employees' passion for the brand. Finally, carving out a personality pulls all the threads together— it tells the customers who you are and what you stand for.

Now that you understand how to build a strong brand, you can go about strengthening your brand through service. Let's consider the FAME approach, which will revolutionize your service strategy and truly set you apart from the crowd.

FAME PART 1
FRAMEWORK

WITHOUT A STRUCTURE to guide your work, it's difficult to advance. If you are writing a book, you need a structure for it—for each chapter, paragraph, and sentence. Structures and frameworks organize our thinking, help us design our next steps, and ultimately guide behaviour. In the business context, successful organizations often adopt "values" as their behaviour framework, which are agreed upon as desirable actions for all employees across the organization.

One of the more famous examples of a successful organization with clear values is Zappos (an online shoe and clothing shop based in Las Vegas, Nevada, which Amazon acquired for $1.2 billion in 2009). Its values are: "Deliver WOW Through Service, Create Fun and a Little Weirdness, Pursue Growth and Learning, Build a Positive Team and Family Spirit, and Be Humble."[1] This framework drives a strong company culture, as it guides Zappos employee behaviour and helps to ensure consistency across the organization.

Without a strong framework, employees often lack a true understanding of the behaviours they should display with each other and with the customer. As Zappos CEO Tony Hsieh states, "It doesn't matter what your company's core values are. What matters is that you have them and that you commit to them. What is important is the alignment that you get from them when they become the default way of think-ing for the entire organization."[2] A compelling, clear, and memorable framework supports consistent behaviour that drives the organization forward.

In Part One, I will present you with a framework that I've used suc-cessfully with many organizations to help guide their service initiatives. One of the reasons why this frame *works* is that it is based on the sci-ence of service, so please join in me the laboratory—but no, you don't need those protective goggles; they look ridiculous on you.

2

Creating a Clear, Compelling, and Memorable Service Framework

"THERE GO OUR rivals," yelled Winton as another bus whisked past as the Kiwi Experience bus approached Franz Josef Glacier. The passengers released a huge "Boooo" and pulled various faces at the competition disappearing in the distance.

"They weren't hanging about," said Rory.

"They have got to get back to Auckland as soon as possible," replied Winton as he eased around another gorgeous curve in the road. "There's no time for the driver to show them the hidden secrets of New Zealand."

"Yeah, right. It's not as if it's important or anything," said Rory and laughed.

Kiwi Experience's market research has shown that the driver makes or breaks a KE trip. The driver delivers on the core promise of the trip: to give backpackers a backstage pass around New Zealand and to create the smoothest trip possible. Of course, a key part of that is safely driving the bus around New Zealand and not treating the trip as if it were a bus rally. This is why KE undertakes a very comprehensive and strict selection process for its drivers.

Drivers must have extensive, safe driving experience. They must be fun, young, and adventurous. They must have an outgoing personality and be proud to show off New Zealand. (Most drivers are from New Zealand but not all.) Kiwi Experience receives hundreds of applications for their driver jobs, because of the company's great reputation. However, very few drivers fit the strict selection criteria. The drivers must undergo a series of driving tests and interviews before they are selected; even then they may not get the job. If selected, they go through a rigorous training program where they learn extensive knowledge about New Zealand and how to make the trip safe and enjoyable at every twist and turn. The drivers are the single most important asset of KE. Their safe driving, knowledge, and personality have a huge impact on customers' perception of the overall quality of the trip and of KE as a whole.

Every positive customer experience is driven first and foremost by being dependable and keeping your core promises. If you can't get the basics right, then any relationship you build will not make the impact it could. Kiwi Experience knows this and it's why they are so particular about hiring the right drivers. Being reliable is not always fun, but it certainly lays the foundation for *having* fun.

The science of service

As I stated in the introduction, this book is based on the science of service. What do I even mean by "science"? Is this just a fancy term to make me seem like a scientist? To make you think I wrote this book while wearing a lab coat and my own safety glasses, shielding me from the flames of my social experiments?

Well yes, but I also mean science as in a "systematically organized body of knowledge on a particular subject that illuminates general truths or highlights the operation of general laws in that subject area."[1] I would like to highlight that there have been many thousands of research papers focused solely on investigating service quality in the eyes of the customer. The science of service is a well-researched and established field, which we need to use.

As the general manager for customer satisfaction at the Commonwealth Bank of Australia, my role was to introduce service research findings to move the organization from the least liked major bank in Australia to the most liked. I went about building a framework linked to important outcomes that would crisply summarize the research on service quality without eliminating its most important elements. Below, I present my four framework insights, using discoveries from the science of service.

Insight #1: All service can be collapsed into the 3Rs

It would have been incredibly difficult to rally the 40,000 employees of the Commonwealth Bank of Australia to deliver better service without a clear, compelling, and memorable framework. The 3Rs enabled me to collapse and summarize my main research findings into three memorable dimensions of service quality: *responsiveness*, *relationships*, and *reliability*.

Ladies and gentlemen, this is the big one! Execute on the 3Rs immediately—before you get distracted by that small banging noise outside and forget what you just read, or you surf the web and find a brilliant recipe for spaghetti with roasted squirrel and start thinking about how you will capture one of those pesky rodents before dinnertime.

Now, let's briefly look at each of these 3Rs.

Responsiveness: It's about speed and positivity, and it's also about keeping the customer informed, giving them cognitive control, reducing customer effort, and showing a willingness to help.

Relationships: Delivering caring, personalized attention to others. It's essentially about asking the customer questions and listening carefully, making them feel important and giving them your undivided attention.

Reliability: The ability to perform the promised service dependably and accurately. Reliability includes educating employees and supporting their ability to convey confidence to and foster trust in the customer. It's about competence, taking ownership, providing a minimum level of quality, and handling customers' problems when they arise.

Much of this book is about deepening our understanding of the 3Rs and how to execute them at the right moment with the customer. Let's further explore the role that the 3Rs play in delivering excellent customer service and how this service drives word-of-mouth positivity.

Insight #2: The 3Rs come in a particular order

Pop quiz! The last thirty years of research into customer service mean not only that we can break down all service into the 3Rs but also that the 3Rs come in a particular order. One of them is always the most important to the customer, one is the second most important, and one is least important. Please remember they are *all* important, but unless you have provided the most important one first, the other do not resonate with a customer.

In which order do customers rank service quality?

A. Relationships, responsiveness, and reliability
B. Responsiveness, reliability, and relationships
C. Reliability, responsiveness, and relationships
D. Relationships, reliability, and responsiveness

If you answer this question right, please send me an email confirming you got the right answer, along with your home address and your bank account details, including your online banking password, and I will ensure there is a significant surprise for you very soon. The email address is 3Rsquizisagiantscam@markcolgate.com

And the right answer is . . .

C.

Fun, right? Sharing the 3Rs and the order in which they come has stuck the most with the companies I have worked with—it is easy to learn, easy to remember, and convincing because it is backed by the science of service.

The importance of reliability

In 2016 the *Harvard Business Review* published a wonderful paper based on the results of research on more than 10,000 U.S. consumers about their perceptions of nearly 50 U.S.-based companies. The authors had this to say about their main finding: "Products and services must attain a certain minimum level, and no other elements can make up for a significant shortfall on this one."[2]

This, of course, is reliability. Other dimensions, like "provides access," "avoids hassles," and "saves time" (all of which are very much like responsiveness) are also prominent in this research, but none of them trump meeting customer expectations on a minimum level of quality. Reliability simply means delivering on your core promises.

Here are some examples of what reliability is and how it outplays everything else.

Table 2.1: Power of reliability

INDUSTRY	WHAT IS MOST IMPORTANT TO YOU?	ASK YOURSELF...
Medical	Correct diagnosis, please.	Would you be happy with a short wait time and a doctor with great bedside manner? Yes... but, oops, they don't diagnose your illness and you stay sick for longer than necessary. What are you thinking now?
Airline	Landing on time (and safely!) at the destination.	You have an easy check-in and great service on the plane, but your flight is delayed two hours due to the pilot being late and you miss your connection. Are you still feeling upbeat?

INDUSTRY	WHAT IS MOST IMPORTANT TO YOU?	ASK YOURSELF...
Hotel	Clean room, peaceful night's sleep.	You stay in a beautiful hotel with personalized, fast service, but the room has a dusty, musty smell and the noise from the street makes it hard to sleep. Does the fact that the valet remembered your name count now?
Consultancy	Gives insights or advice that your company can use.	A consultant engages you and keeps you informed, building a strong relationship, but their insights and advice don't quite hit the mark. Would you use them again?
Mobile phone carrier	Consistent network to make calls and access data services.	How much do you like dropped calls or, worse, no Snapchat connection?
Restaurant	The quality of food.	You're seated at an awesome table near the window, enjoying exquisite service from the waiter, but the food leaves a bad taste in your mouth. How do you feel about that bill now?
University	The quality of the education.	Would you prefer a friendly professor who is always organized or one who seems scattered but provides deeper learning?
Massage	The quality of treatment.	The massage does not live up to expectations, but the RMT is personable and even goes five minutes beyond the treatment time. Would you still be happy with the experience?
Landscaping	The superiority of workmanship.	Would you want a landscaper who is approachable and completes work on time, but the garden does not look how you hoped or outlined in the plans?

Note that for many services, unresponsiveness means that the service may slip into an unreliable territory. If you have to wait so long on hold with a call centre that you give up trying to talk to someone, or if a realtor takes so long to list and sell your house that you miss out on buying another one, well, that is unreliable. Generally, though, most responsiveness is not so extreme.

The point here is that if you are dedicating resources (and we always have limited resources) to being responsive and building strong relationships, but you have not conquered the art of being as reliable as humanly possible, then the responsiveness and the relationships pieces will never land as well as you would like. They simply won't get the shine they deserve.

If you invest time and energy into making sure you are always reliable in terms of accuracy, keeping your key promises, demonstrating competency to build trust, and handling customers' complaints expertly, then the efficiency with which you deliver the service and the personalization of the experience for the customer will have its maximum impact.

What about the other 2Rs?

The research shows that responsiveness is more important than relationships.[3] Think about what is more important to you: fast and efficient service where you are informed along the way and service employees are willing to answer questions you have, or personalized service that is effortful and slow. Slow and inefficient service gets in the way of the impact of personalization and will prevent your organization from moving forward.

Let's look at this a little bit more closely. What difference does it really make to be reliable and responsive and build strong relationships? How do these pieces come together and, most importantly, how do they drive recommendations from one customer to another potential customer?

Insight #3: Great service exponentially drives recommendations

Another revelation that emerged from the service literature was that recommendations from one customer to another, like repeat purchases, are not a linear function. Good service and moderate levels of satisfaction make little impact on a customer's willingness to recommend or repeat purchases. Only exceptional levels of service and very high levels of satisfaction encourage the customer to tell others about their amazing experience with you and to buy again.

Xerox was the first company to research the power of world-class service, relative to moderate levels of service. Xerox discovered that customers who gave them five out of five for service were six times more likely to repurchase Xerox equipment than those giving four out of five.[4] This analysis led Xerox to "extend its efforts to create apostles"—a term coined by Scott D. Cook, CEO of software producer and distributor of Intuit, describing customers so satisfied that they convert the uninitiated to a product or service.[5]

Moving from a one to four (on the five-point scale) doesn't get you much in terms of loyalty; the impact of moving from four to five is nothing short of phenomenal. The Institute of Customer Service in the U.K. did a deep investigation (42,500 responses) into customer service in 2017. They created a U.K. customer satisfaction index (UKCSI) that shows how companies move from good to great (see figure 2.2): "Achieving a customer satisfaction score of nine or ten (out of ten) appears to give a significant boost, compared even to an eight out of ten, to ratings for trust, reputation, intention to remain with an organisation and likelihood to recommend."[6]

Enterprise Rent-A-Car's research resulted in a very similar statistic to Xerox's and UKCSI's research. Enterprise CEO Andy Taylor points out its key discovery that "top box customers were more than three times as likely to use Enterprise again as those who were somewhat satisfied." Taylor continues, "We then checked customers' intentions against their actual behavior to see whether, in fact, they did rent from us again. And we found that they did indeed. We now had hard proof that a high ESQi [the Enterprise service quality index, which translates to customer satisfaction] score translated into real dollars of revenue and profit. Much of the internal grumbling we had been hearing about ESQi began to quiet considerably, because the system had really begun to prove its value to our bottom-line operators."[7]

Figure 2.2: The impact of moving from good to great

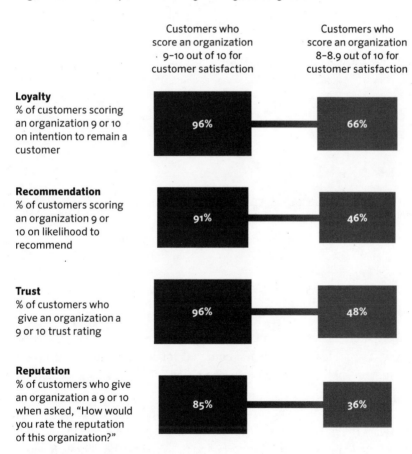

Customers who score an organization 9–10 out of 10 for customer satisfaction

Customers who score an organization 8–8.9 out of 10 for customer satisfaction

Loyalty
% of customers scoring an organization 9 or 10 on intention to remain a customer

96%   66%

Recommendation
% of customers scoring an organization 9 or 10 on likelihood to recommend

91%   46%

Trust
% of customers who give an organization a 9 or 10 trust rating

96%   48%

Reputation
% of customers who give an organization a 9 or 10 when asked, "How would you rate the reputation of this organization?"

85%   36%

Source: U.K. Institute of Customer Satisfaction[8]

While I was working at Commonwealth Bank, we read a report that surveyed 22,000 customers around the world who were asked to rate a service company they regularly did business with on a scale from one to ten in terms of overall customer service (X axis) and compare this rating to their likelihood to recommend (Y axis). See figure 2.3.

Figure 2.3: Overall customer service rating and likelihood to recommend

Service excellence and customer advocates

Source: Nielsen Research[9]

One out of ten for service meant you hated the company and were likely a terrorizing customer, sniping them at every opportunity. However, if you rated them ten, it meant that you loved them and you want to marry employees from the organization—they are that good at looking after you.

The number that appears above the customer service rating on the X axis is the percentage of respondents in each category who said that they would recommend this company to someone they knew. It was a simple yes or no question.

So, for example, if you look at the seven rating for overall service—a good rating—21 percent of customers said yes, they would recommend that company to someone they knew. For the three rating, only 4 percent of customers would recommend that company. But with a nine rating—a great rating—89 percent of customers would recommend that company.

There are two incredible findings from this research. First, look at the difference between a seven and a nine. Providing great levels of service will get nine out of ten customers to recommend you, but providing good levels of service (seven out of ten) gets you hardly anywhere. Remember that most service organizations rely heavily on word-of-mouth from one customer to another potential customer, so understanding that only excellent service drives recommendations is critical. While the eight rating does pretty well in terms of recommendations, there is still a leap from eight to nine, which is why we should focus on the very highest levels of service.

The second critical finding is that the worse the service gets, the more likely you are to get recommendations! As you go from a three for service to two to one, you get more and more recommendations. This is hard to explain, but I reckon it's pretty straightforward: customers recommend companies they hate to people they hate: "Definitely get a Starbucks, Bob; their coffee is delicious." Actually, what is likely going on is that responders misinterpreted this question to mean "their service is so bad that I recommend friends or colleagues *don't* use them."

Research company Forrester discovered that the non-linearity of the service/recommendation line means that investing in moving people from the six-to-eight range to a nine or ten will provide 8.8 times more revenue than moving people from one end of the scale to the middle of the scale.[10] That is something all leaders should know. Further, there are *dramatically* more people in the "feeling positive" category (sevens and eights) than in the negative end of the scale, so we can boost more revenue per customer *and* reach more people at the same time.[11]

Insight #4: Overlaying 3Rs onto the recommendation insight

I know the last three insights have left you completely overwhelmed with excitement, but before you lie down with a damp copy of *The Economist* on your face, I have one more insight for you.

When we mapped the 3Rs onto this research, we learned that if the organization could not deliver on its core promises, then customers rated it to the far left of the scale. If a grocery delivery doesn't arrive in time for dinner, or a lawyer's advice backfires, or a car mechanic doesn't fix the problem, then a customer rates the service on the one-to-four end of the scale.

Figure 2.4: Overlaying 3Rs with recommendations

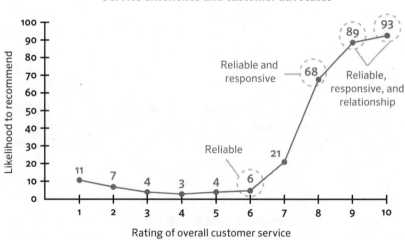

Service excellence and customer advocates

If a customer finds a firm to be reliable but not responsive and poor at relationship building, then the company gets rated around a six or seven on the scale. You've done the most basic service right but not with efficiency or friendliness.

If the customer felt the company was reliable and responsive but missed the mark in terms of personalization, then they mostly rated the company an eight. There was still something missing. In some cases, being reliable and responsive led to a nine or ten. If the customer was in a hurry, or not interested in building a relationship, then being reliable and responsive was enough to create a very satisfying experience.

If you were reliable, responsive, *and* you built a relationship, the customers would virtually always rate you a nine or ten. The finding, illustrated in figure 2.4, is gold.

Even though I've been downplaying the importance of relationships throughout most of this chapter, the reality is that relationship building is the great differentiator. Many organizations are reliable and responsive, but if you really want to be a world-class organization that always delivers fantastic service, then being reliable, responsive, *and* building a strong relationship will set you apart.

CASE STUDY: The Whistler Experience

NOW, LET'S LOOK at the town of Whistler, BC. In 2014, the whole town and all the organizations within it were looking to rally around world-class service, and they came knocking on my door for help. The Whistler Experience shows that with a simple framework based on science, a visionary Chamber of Commerce, and some incredibly eager business participants, you can achieve almost anything.

History

In 1986, the Whistler Chamber of Commerce reached out to Whistler Tourism to initiate a customer service program for the community. From the beginning, the vision was to turn customer service into a competitive advantage for the Whistler resort. From 1987 to 2014, the Sprint Program grew into a community offering with annual service training and a better understanding of the resort for new employees.

Even though enrollment was high, the program lacked ongoing inspiration and events were perceived as one-off. While the local leadership enjoyed learning from high-calibre guest speakers, post-event guidance was missing and business owners were unmotivated to make changes to achieve better or maintain consistent service levels. Additionally, the majority of longer-term employees perceived the training as repetitive and without depth.

That's why, in 2013–14, the chamber underwent a comprehensive review process with resort partners and the business community. The community asked for three things to rejuvenate Whistler's service program: inspiring speakers, world-class content, and implementable tools.

Pilot workshop

In January 2014, the chamber's CEO, Val Litwin, reached out to Saul Klein, the dean of the University of Victoria's Peter B. Gustavson School of Business. Together, they explored the opportunity of bringing executive-style education on service excellence to the resort of Whistler.

To test the waters, I delivered the first workshop in Whistler in March 2014. I spoke on the 3Rs and how to execute them every day. As Litwin says, "Our attendance goal was forty. In the end, we had 136 people. Their feedback was outstanding and confirmed that we had found an expert community partner with Gustavson School of Business."

Start and takeoff

Building on the success of the pilot workshop, the Whistler Chamber rebranded its service excellence program as The Whistler Experience. Today The Whistler Experience embraces all chamber initiatives that elevate service in Whistler.

The Whistler Experience is a service solution that teaches teams how to plan for and deliver powerful experiences that customers won't stop talking about. From the beginning, the Whistler Chamber of Commerce recognized that training outcomes will only last if backed up with implementation programs like the secret shopper program, which offers service feedback to employers and employees.

The initial success was essential to boost the confidence and funding levels of the municipality, the resort partners (Whistler Blackcomb, Tourism Whistler), and sponsors.

Why did the community buy into The Whistler Experience?

The community united behind the 3Rs for three reasons:

1. Thanks to the innovative partnership with the Gustavson School of Business, the Whistler Experience offers leading-edge content based on science, presented by a highly engaging team of experts. The core framework is based on social psychology and explains what people value in their service experiences.
2. The program included relevant implementation tools for all employees, including handouts, the secret shopper program, and an implementation guide. For example, the secret shopper program is probably the single most effective tool a business can apply after training is completed, as it takes the temperature of current service levels and provides material for coaching sessions.
3. The Whistler community acknowledges that a rising tide lifts all boats. They endorse the program's vision to become the number one resort town in the world for service—a commitment to consistently provide high service levels.

After the first series of training courses, highly engaged businesses from the town of Whistler met with me every month to discuss execution. They wanted a simple framework to teach their employees. That's when the group decided that the 3Rs—the three things customers are looking for in any service interaction—should become Whistler's service values. This focus generated a new wave of interest in The Whistler Experience, as the 3Rs are easy to explain and to remember. The 3Rs are now the starting point of any service conversation in team meetings, one-on-one coaching sessions, or recognition initiatives.

Success breeds success

In its first three months in 2014, the program saw more than 5,000 participants—a diverse group of front-liners, supervisors, managers, and partners from Whistler and beyond. Within two and a half years, more than 16,000 have learned about the 3Rs. This is very impressive for a community with a permanent population of approximately 10,000 people.

Key Whistler businesses—large and small—adopted the framework, including Whistler Blackcomb, The Mexican Corner, Canadian Wilderness Adventures, and Gibbons Hospitality.

In its third year, word-of-mouth spread beyond the resort in the hospitality sector. In 2017, more than 200 company representatives made the trip to Whistler to learn about the 3RS, moments of power (see Part Three of this book), and how to implement a service culture to cultivate their own brand.

Barrett Fisher, president and CEO of Tourism Whistler, says, "Throughout winter 2015–16 and 2016–2017 and summer 2016 and 2017, Whistler served more guests than ever. Still, thousands of guests rated Whistler's service *higher* than in the past. Our community has every reason to be proud of the 3RS."

Where is The Whistler Experience going from here?

The 3RS and moments of power are the foundations of The Whistler Experience. Introductory courses help to build common understanding and language. Leadership courses are offered to help leaders implement a true service culture.

Mechthild Facundo, the GM of The Whistler Experience, says, "We take pride in offering leading-edge training *plus* implementation tools. Everybody loves inspiring training, but that's the first step. The second step is to help organizations build their service brand. We break it down to a few simple steps to create a true service culture. Our message is clear: nothing will improve unless management declares service a competitive advantage, sets service goals, and coaches each employee accordingly."

The Whistler Experience fosters a dedication to make Whistler renowned as the best place to ski and ride in North America, and it's become the best resort for employees to learn about service. Why would you work anywhere else if you can learn crucial business skills and earn a certificate all while having fun?

Facundo adds, "The Whistler Experience has grown into a community movement. In less than three years, the vast majority of organizations sing off the same song sheet."

The 3Rs and The Whistler Experience have been a great mix of science and engaging content, with the Whistler Chamber of Commerce acting as the facilitator for local businesses. This facilitation role helps businesses execute great service with their customers. The vision of the Chamber to train a whole town is a bold one, but with the right approach, partnerships, and a focus on execution, they've shown it can be done!

Recap

Here are the four main insights related to building a framework that supports your brand and customer service.

1. The 3Rs of reliability, responsiveness, and relationships summarize all you need to know about delivering service.
2. The 3Rs come in a particular order. Reliability, then responsiveness, and then the customers say they are wide open to the relationship.
3. Recommendations are driven by great service, not good service— the difference between a seven and a nine out of ten is critical.
4. You can overlay 3Rs onto the likelihood-to-recommend scale (figure 2.3) and see how they build on each other. Relationships drive nines and tens, but only when reliability and responsiveness are also present.

Use the science of service to your advantage. Set yourself apart by designing your service around frameworks based on research. I have seen how employees, firms, and even towns rally around the 3Rs, because it is a clear, compelling, and memorable framework. If you don't have a service framework embedded in your workplace, give the 3Rs a chance. While nothing in life is guaranteed, the probability is that this framework will make a difference.

RANDOM STORY:
Great Service in Canada Is So Easy

CANADIANS ARE SOME of the friendliest and politest people on the planet. I believe that, as a result, service is easier for them than for others. But I am sure you are wondering, just how friendly are they really?

Well, as you know, I have been working in Whistler for a few years and I have done some exploring. One of the more famous places around there is Lost Lake, a ten-minute walk or a few minutes' cycle from the heart of Whistler Village. Lost Lake is amazing for walking and for cycling. While cycling on one of my first trips there, I came across this sign. It is a real sign. There's no Photoshop done here, folks.

What the sign says is that if you are a cyclist, you should yield to hikers meandering around the trails. Fair enough, don't you think?

The sign also says that if you are a cyclist or walker, you should give way to a bear. Now, this sign is ludicrous for two reasons. One, can you imagine any scenario where a hiker would barge in front of the way of a bear shouting, "Get out of the way, fuzzy one; I'm first!"? And if the hiker/cyclist is willing to push the bear out of the way, well, they deserve to be mangled and eaten, don't you think? And for that second reason, the sign is implausible.

However, this sums up Canadians: they are so friendly that they just want everyone to play fair and let the bears go first. I don't believe you would see this sign in any other country. In Australia, for example, there would be a picture of you wrestling with the local dangerous animal to encourage interaction with the wildlife.

Canadians are so friendly that there is even a group of activists petitioning for bears to be given weapons to protect themselves from humans, as their natural habitat is ever decreasing. This gives me a perfect way of describing the difference between Americans and Canadians. Americans believe in the right to bear arms, while Canadians believe in the right to arm bears.

FAME PART 2
ACCOUNTABILITY

THE HOLY GRAIL of any corporate culture is accountability. It's a potent moment when an employee feels an acute sense of responsibility and ownership to help the company achieve its strategic goals.

You can't tell employees to be accountable, because they will reject the assertion and probably make a memorable hand gesture in your direction. But you can build accountability in ways that are meaningful to them.

Successful service companies hardwire accountability in employees. They show employees that the company's sense of purpose aligns with theirs; they enable them to self-direct their own work rather than micromanaging them; they reward and recognize great service in ways that are consequential, not superficial. They coach and mentor employees to reach their potential, so employees feel a sense of progress in their roles and careers—which engrains accountability even more. Who doesn't want to help an organization achieve its goals when it is also helping you achieve yours?

In the hotel industry, Ritz-Carlton, a subsidiary of Marriott International Inc., is known for its fixation on customer metrics and process improvements. From a customer point of view, Ritz-Carlton employees seem to be naturally extraordinary at personalized service, but the reality is that the company has created a comprehensive service system. This system includes extensive onboarding and ongoing training programs, strong leaders who mentor employees as well as walking the talk, and policies and processes that reward employees for going above and beyond to delight guests. These approaches build accountability.

Most of you can think of at least one organization that has been so consistently impressive, you've been compelled to tell your family and friends about it. Behind this great service, there's a clear vision, strong leadership, and a perfect balance of goals, people, and effective processes. That is, the service system has been carefully designed to build in accountability and ensure the organization's goals are met.

What you see in these firms is not an accident; its employees are taking ownership of the customer experience because they literally feel like they own it. The customer experience *is* the employee experience, and the employee feels a sense of pride when they deliver consistently on the customer experience. This service experience ultimately builds strong relationships. Where accountability is lacking, employees often attempt to boost their self-esteem by putting customers down, ignoring customer complaints, or delivering service that matches their mood at the time. Instead, they could be performing at a high level with every customer in every interaction.

Sounds idealistic, doesn't it? You're right; it is ideal—so let's see how it is done.

3

Designing a
Service System

"**S**o HOW DO you keep your energy up every day, every trip?" Rory asked Winton, who looked tired at the end of a long driving day.

"I get lots of breaks, so that helps," said Winton. "We don't often do two trips back to back, but even when we do, we are always given feedback from the passengers at the end of every trip—good or bad. This feedback comes through the bus survey we do in Queenstown and any social media postings. It always keeps it real and refreshes us."

"Well, I have some feedback for you," said Rory.

"I'm all ears," said Winton.

"You've split some coffee on your T-shirt," said Rory.

"And you've got most of your lunch on your shirt," said Winton.

Surprised, Rory looked down to inspect, as Winton said, "Kidding. We aren't always as respectful to our customers as we should be."

"That's going on my survey," replied Rory.

Kiwi Experience has carefully built a system where they routinely create accountability and deliver on passengers' needs. To do this, they ensure employees (drivers, front-line staff, and back-office staff) understand the service concept. Leaders then create interventions so employees have an acute understanding of what customers want on an ongoing basis.

First, they undertook research to truly understand their target market. Then they shared the findings with every employee.

> [Our customers are] 18–35-year-old men and women. They have a sense of anticipation; they crave the unknown and are seeking total adventure. The thought of meeting new people is an essential criteria in their choice of holiday... They spend time wondering what the dynamic of the group might be, and the "unknown" is a thrill for them. They are free of the day-to-day rat race and they yearn to be their hedonistic selves. Each day is a new feeling, a new experience... There is little time for thinking on this holiday, only time for doing! These men and women love a laugh—they love the sensation of not taking anything too seriously (there will be other times in their life when they will have to be grown-up)... Right now, life is about living—to the max.

By sharing with employees this target-market profile and continually highlighting how the KE concept can meet these needs, leaders tighten expectations around the role each employee plays and what success looks like.

Second, KE surveys every customer on every bus. One of the directors and the operations manager read all the surveys to monitor what is happening. They then use these surveys to improve their service to the marketplace, understanding which drivers are performing and which ones are not meeting expectations. Although the KE core experience has basically stayed the same, they try to add value to their service through continuous improvements based on customer feedback.

Third, KE tries to get *everyone* in the business interacting with customers. For example, there was a barbecue at a backpacker hostel in Auckland recently at which KE had their accountants and other staff meet the guests. Those staff members do not usually come in direct contact with customers, but this event gave them a better understanding of who KE's customers are and where they come from.

Fourth, after each trip, an operations manager debriefs the driver to understand how tired they are, and whether they should be taken off the duty roster for a couple of weeks. An exhausted driver cannot provide the best service for the customers, and this would only harm the reputation of both the driver and KE in the long run. An experienced operations manager can easily spot when a driver needs rest. The drivers are also required to fill out a survey at the end of each trip that asks them how the trip went and any problems they encountered. The survey includes a section for the driver to make recommendations to improve the overall quality of KE.

In summary, KE has hardwired accountability more than most organizations I have worked with by:

- having a clear service concept,
- having an acute understanding of its market,
- having continual measurements in place to track the quality of the experience and the performance of the drivers,
- ensuring *all* employees meet the customer—so they can feel a real sense of who they're serving,
- and engaging in recurrent research with drivers to understand their energy levels and their suggestions for what could be improved.

With accountability hardwired and a strong service system, your company will be much more likely to deliver a continually memorable experience.

Creating accountable service

For accountability to be built within every employee, two things need to happen. First, a strong service system needs to be built *across* the organization. The strength of this service system will determine much of the ownership that employees feel. But this is not enough. Second, every *individual* team and employee must have a clear understanding of the expectations that leaders have of them; they must feel empowered to deliver on these expectations; and they must receive high-quality feedback, so they can continually grow and act autonomously. Unless we bring accountability to the individual level, the service system will never achieve its full effect. Conversely, creating buy-in at the individual level is unlikely to be sustainable unless the service system reinforces this ownership.

First, let's explore how to create accountability across the organization.

The strength of the service system

In my first year as the GM of customer satisfaction at the Commonwealth Bank of Australia, I helped to redesign the service system and how the pieces of the service puzzle connect. After we designed this system, my last two years were spent getting my hands dirty and helping execute the system on the front line, particularly in the call centres, branches, and the private bank (for very high net worth clients only; please note there was no danger of me getting on their list). The call centres and branches were spread all over Australia, so much of my time was spent fighting off koalas and snakes as I travelled the country. I also could have achieved so much more had I not been running from spiders every twenty minutes or so.

Before we dig into the Commonwealth Bank of Australia case, let's examine the key elements of a system that enables accountability across an organization.

A strong service system has four parts. First, there needs to be a clear service strategy and concept. Think Kiwi Experience, T-Mobile, or Salesforce. Ultimately, there should be a clear strategy in respect to the purpose of delivering service, with all employees understanding and finding meaning in it.

Second, this vision must be measurable, with, for instance, a customer scorecard (see an example on my website: markcolgate.com), to continually ensure you are fulfilling the target market's needs. In this respect, you need to know, with clarity, who your target market is and what their needs are, and then you can track your ability to continually deliver on those needs. Employees who are delivering service need to know the score; games change when a score is kept and it's not a subtle change.

Figure 3.1: The design of a strong service system

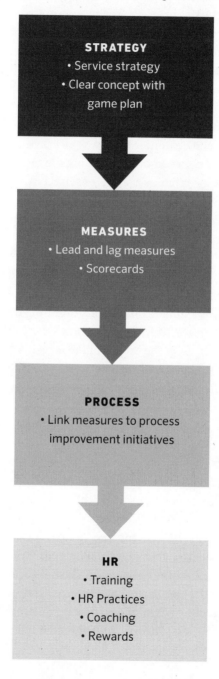

Third, you need to design the operating system so that you can continually improve your processes based on the feedback you get from the customer scorecards. Once you understand which areas your business is meeting (or that you are exceeding customers' expectations), you need to zero in on those processes that are *not* meeting customer expectations. In this respect, the customer scorecards are always driving the process improvements, rather than you picking processes that you believe you should be improving. Employees can see the link between customer feedback and process improvements. A tight connection between understanding the target market's needs and improving process builds a stronger service system.

The final element of a strong service system is where your vision, your customer scorecards, and your process improvements are linked to your HR system. For example, employees are recognized and rewarded for delivering excellence or exceeding goals in relation to customer feedback. Hiring is built on an acute understanding of which employees are most suitable given the service concept. The Kiwi Experience case study is a great example of integrating the service system with HR. The drivers were hired on the company's explicit understanding of applicant "fit" with the target market's needs.

You must aim to excel in all parts of the service system. The fun part here is that you likely have most of these elements already operating inside your organization, and, in many cases, you simply need to put the pieces of the puzzle together, so that employees can understand how the whole system is interconnected.

However, some key parts could be missing—for example, you might not have detailed customer scorecards that enable you to understand where you're falling short, or maybe the vision needs some work in terms of refining your service concept.

These are building blocks: you need a clear service strategy before you can carefully detail your customer scorecards. Otherwise, you'll be collecting customer feedback and measures of performance that are not strategically connected to the organization. Without clear customer scorecards, you might be picking and redesigning service processes that are less critical from the customer's point of view.

The framework of the 3Rs—reliability, responsiveness, and relationships—enables you to immediately understand which needs are most important and build from there.

HR processes are the final level, after you have a clear understanding of your service strategy, you have articulated your customers' needs through metrics and feedback, and you have linked these metrics to process improvements. Then you can appropriately coach, recognize, reward, hire, orientate, and conduct useful performance reviews because you know what type of employees you need and how you need them to perform. A strong service system promotes a strong HR system, and vice versa.

THE WRONG KIND OF ACCOUNTABILITY

GIVEN THAT I teach customer service, I have been exposed to the most amazing service stories involving employees taking accountability. However, not all accountability behaviours are the right ones.

One of my favourite bad ones came from an executive I taught recently. He was flying with a North American airline that will remain nameless, and his flight had taken off late with passengers given no updates. When he asked one of the flight attendants what time the plane would land, she replied, quite incredibly, "How would I know? I don't have a glass ball." He was flabbergasted. Why was she so rude? Surely, she should know the time that they're supposed to land? Two minutes later she came back down the aisle to see him.

He thought, *Here we go, she has come to take accountability and apologize for being so abrupt with me.* She walked over and leaned in to speak to him. "I'm sorry," she said. "I didn't mean to say glass ball, I meant crystal ball. I don't have a crystal ball to tell you what time the plane will arrive, because I'm not a fortune teller."

I've heard many more that are as bad, believe it or not!

Fortunately, I've also heard many amazing stories of heroic service where the employee takes ownership. The best story I've heard was about a competitor in an Ironman race staying in a local hotel. At the end of the race—before the participant came back to the hotel room—a hotel service representative found out the contestant's finishing time. They ordered a small cake with the time iced on top and left it in the contestant's room. Imagine how special and appreciated you would feel when you found that cake waiting for you.

My own personal experience of amazing customer service happened at a nearby restaurant. The server was very friendly from the moment we walked in, but things got interesting once the meal started. The server came over, placed the appetizer down, and lightly flicked my hair as they left. Then, during the main course, the server put the entrée in front of me and tweaked my shoulder, in a pleasant way. And then, when dessert was served, the server brushed my ear with their thumb. That's when I realized the difference between good service and great service—it's those little touches.

Level 1: Service strategy

Service strategy is the foundation, your game plan—the footing to drive meaning at work and to guide all subsequent service efforts.

You must diagnose the situation you are in (by analyzing your current service strengths and weaknesses and understanding how you can differentiate yourself from the competition) and make clear choices about what you can and cannot do for the customer. (Again, think Salesforce: "We don't do software.") Then you need to craft your customer experience strategy, aligning it with the company's overall strategy and brand, and then share that strategy with employees to guide decision-making and prioritization across the organization.

The service strategy defines the intended experience. For example, the experience at Costco—a warehouse store where customers push oversized carts through huge aisles stacked high with value-priced products—is very different from the experience at an Apple store, where customers see a comparatively sparse selection of pricey products and receive expert assistance. Costco's experience aligns with its overall strategy as a cost leader; Apple's aligns with its strategy of innovation.

A clear service strategy is the critical blueprint for the experience you then design, deliver, manage, and measure (levels 2–4). Without it, you, your employees, and your other stakeholders won't know whether to deliver an experience like the one at Costco, at Apple, or somewhere else entirely.

Level 2: Measurement

Measurement is critical. The measurement level requires a set of practices so organizations can quantify the quality of customer experience in a consistent manner and deliver actionable insights to employees. If you are not measuring what customers' experiences of service, you will run into many problems. You won't be able to track progress—and nothing drives your ability to create service FAME than evidence that what you are doing is working.

Beyond showing the progress you are making—or lack thereof—a scorecard helps enormously because it identifies which aspects of the customer experience drive the overall experience the most. With that insight, you can then carefully prioritize what is most important from the customers' point of view and identify which measures you should pay the most attention to.

At this juncture, it is important to distinguish between lag and lead measures on a scorecard.[1] A lag measure is a measurement of a result you are trying to achieve. They are called lag measures because by the time you get the data, the result has already happened; they are always lagging. Lead measures are different; they forecast the result. They have two primary characteristics.[2] First, a lead measure is predictive, meaning that if the lead measure changes, you can predict that the lag measure will also change. Second, a lead measure can be directly influenced by the employee or team. In short, lag measures are metrics, but lead measures are actions.

Let's explore the two characteristics of a good lead service measure. Let's say your goal, as a mobile phone company, is to reduce customer defection. A lag measure would be to reduce churn (customer exit) by 2 percent per month to 1.5 percent per month. A lead measure would be the first-call resolution in the call centre or customers perceiving personal attention in a service interaction. Both of these are predictive and can be influenced.

Another example is waiting time in retail stores or in call centres. This is a lag measure: while it is important, it cannot be influenced. What would influence waiting time is the number of representatives in the stores or call centre and the efficiency of handling customer inquiries, for example. These are actions that can affect waiting time. Your scorecard should include important lag measures—to track how are you are doing—but should be mostly driven by a set of lead measures, which everyone feels they can influence. Everyone should understand the lead measures drive the important lag measures.

A fantastic example of a company that has the first two levels spot-on is Enterprise Rent-A-Car. More than sixty years ago, Jack Taylor founded Enterprise Rent-A-Car on a simple philosophy: "Take care of your customers and your employees first, and the profits will follow." This consistent approach has led it to unparalleled success in terms of growth and customer satisfaction. It is now the biggest car rental company in the world with more than one million cars in its fleet and nearly 100,000 employees. Over 80 percent of customers state they are completely satisfied. Enterprise was rated, for the fourth year in a row, as number one in the J.D. Power 2017 North America Rental Car Satisfaction Study.

Early on, Enterprise Rent-A-Car realized it could not be all things to all people, so it focused on very tight target markets, which were not served by other rental companies; essentially, it made a choice about who it should and should not serve. As Michael Porter, the strategy guru, states, "The essence of strategy is choosing what not to do."

Figure 3.2 shows the clear choice Enterprise Rent-A-Car made in terms of its target markets.

Figure 3.2: Enterprise Rent-A-Car target markets

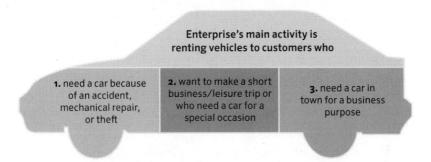

Enterprise's main activity is renting vehicles to customers who

1. need a car because of an accident, mechanical repair, or theft

2. want to make a short business/leisure trip or who need a car for a special occasion

3. need a car in town for a business purpose

Source: Business Case studies[3]

Arguably just as important as this focused approach was the company's commitment to the Enterprise Service Quality Index (ESQi). Every month, around 200,000 Enterprise Rent-A-Car customers are asked to rate the service they received on a five-point scale from completely dissatisfied (one) to completely satisfied (five). This rating is the basis for measuring the performance of all Enterprise rental branches (and National and Alamo branches, subsidiaries of Enterprise). The main metric is the number of fives a branch receives (i.e., "completely satisfied" customers), because, as noted in Insight #3 in chapter 2, customers who are completely satisfied are three times more likely to rent again than customers who are only somewhat satisfied (four out of five). This clear metric impacts employee behaviours and financial rewards.

The ESQi results have helped to teach Enterprise which three factors (lead measures) create very high levels of customer satisfaction:

- the cleanliness of the car (reliability),
- the speed of the transaction (responsiveness), and
- the attitude and helpfulness of Enterprise employees (relationship building).

ESQi is regarded as fundamental to the company's values. Enterprise employees at branch manager level and above have their ESQi scores taken into consideration when it comes to career advancement, ensuring that employees' success is linked to outstanding service. It's a central part of Enterprise's corporate culture.[4]

One big advantage of Enterprise's business model is that the decentralized structure gives employees a lot of room to make the right actions for their customers autonomously—in other words, they have accountability. This approach aids and encourages employees to really make a difference when dealing with every single customer.

Level 3: Processes

It's important to link the results from your lead measures to improvements in your processes. Lead measures tell you which things to fix immediately (severe process problems), which to improve over time (less critical processes that are broken, or critical process that are slowly diminishing in quality), which to maintain at current levels, and which to promote as strengths (important dimensions of the customer experience which you are delivering expertly and which differentiate you from the competition).

Without connecting measurement (level 2) to process (level 3), you may be redesigning processes that are not the most important. Prioritize the service actions that are crucial from the customer's point of view. Also, if you know what the customers' priorities are but don't have consistently collected data, then you do not have the evidence to persuade the leaders to invest in these processes.

As an example, I worked for an insurance company where we built a customer scorecard, but the firm was not collecting any customer satisfaction data on the claims process. Clearly, the claims process in an insurance context is a critical service interaction, and if you're not collecting any service data, you are unlikely to improve it. You might end up focusing on other, less important processes. We tend to overlook or undervalue feedback on the most important aspects and processes of our business.

The idea here is that there is a logic that employees can buy into. You have a clear customer experience strategy, defined by clear metrics that are important from the customer's point of view. You have identified not only the key lag measures but also the lead measures that drive these important outcomes. You have connected the feedback on these measures to drive process improvements, so that employees understand why you are investing in redesigning this process—because it will have a significant and positive impact on the customer experience.

To make accountability even more engrained, we connect levels 1, 2, and 3 with HR practices.

Level 4: HR

You will reach the highest level of sophistication when you link your first three levels to HR practices. In a service context, the employees deliver the gold. The more HR practices are seen to be driven by a clear and coherent service system, the more likely it is that employees will be receptive to HR's policies and practices.

As we will talk about extensively in the final chapter of this book, the critical HR practice is coaching (also the subject of my first book, *8 Moments of Power in Coaching*[5]). Great service will only be sustained if employees are coached to raise their service performance on a consistent basis. Without this coaching and feedback, employee performance will plateau. However, this coaching must have context. Which behaviours are we looking for the employees to improve on? Which behaviours make a difference from the customer's point of view? How does the coaching link to the customer measures on the scorecard? For example, if customer feedback tells you that the customer complaint process is weak and you decide to invest in this process, then the subsequent coaching needs to revolve around this redesigned process, so employees can execute it expertly.

Hiring, orientation, and performance reviews should also revolve around employees meeting customer service expectations. The clearer the customer experience strategy and the sharper you have detailed the target market's needs, the more you can drive the HR system forward.

Finally, it is important to highlight the importance of recognition and rewards in the service equation. The more methodical you are at recognizing and rewarding employees who meet or exceed customers' expectations based on measures within your customer scorecard (for example, Enterprise Rent-A-Car only promoted employees who did well on ESQi), the more likely you are to sustain motivation within the organization. The opposite approach—rewarding employees for other priorities (such as sales)—sends out a very strong message in terms of what you *really* believe in, and it's harmful to the overall organization.

Your service system creates disciplines

Ultimately, your service system sets up habits that enable you to always deliver great service. These habits push us through when we experience setbacks, are disillusioned, or tempted to focus on other things. I have identified seven key disciplines that can be applied to your service plan, or really to any goal you might have—professionally or personally. These are: clear goal, framework, measurement, redesign, coach, commitments, recognize and reward.

Table 3.1 outlines the top seven disciplines a service system creates. I have compared the disciplines needed for a service system to the ones you need to become a great distance runner. We all know you can't become a great runner without clear habits—well, great service is the same, but we tend not to make that connection. With every habit you put in place, your chance of building your service FAME increases. However, if you implement only one habit, your chances go down. The same applies to running. While there are no guarantees in life (in running, you may get injured; in business, you may get a new CEO who takes the firm in a whole new direction), these disciplines set you up for success.

Table 3.1: Top seven disciplines of the service system

TOP SEVEN DISCIPLINES	RUNNING	SERVICE
1. Clear Goal: Have clear goals for what you are trying to achieve.	The date of a race, the time you want to run, etc.	Craft a customer experience goal that is specific, measurable, and time-bound.
2. Framework: Use a structure to achieve your strategy.	Type of training runs (e.g., sprints, hill training), the frequency of runs each week, etc.	Outline a structured guide to help employees deliver great service (e.g., the framework of the 3Rs and their associated priorities).
3. Measurement: Track your progress and score.	Track your running progress; identify key roadblocks to improvement.	Collect and share customer feedback on key lead and lag metrics to show how you can advance.
4. Redesign: Alter your plan as things change.	Alter your running plan to adjust to injuries, feedback from coach, etc.	Drive continual improvement by redesigning processes based on customer feedback from the scorecard.
5. Commitments: Create better habits to help you achieve your goal.	Implement habits such as changing your diet, use a running app, etc.	Build weekly service meetings to deepen attention to service. Collect and share customer experiences every day.
6. Coach: Use a coach to drive performance to another level.	Find a coach and/or a group to run with (they will motivate you and are a support group).	Provide continual feedback, support, and encouragement to employees, through a coach, to help them raise their game.
7. Recognize and Reward: Celebrate success at every level.	Take days off, treat yourself when you have achieved goals, and celebrate with others in your running group.	Recognize great service by rewarding employees or have systematic and meaningful ways to acknowledge success.

Employee and team level integration: Tight-loose-tight

Once you have designed and executed a service system, you are a long way down the path to hardwiring accountability into the whole organization. However, each employee does not yet have a personal sense of accountability. The next critical step is to institutionalize a tight-loose-tight system, as illustrated in figure 3.3.

Figure 3.3: The continuous loop of tight-loose-tight

A. Team members are given a clear vision, goal(s), expectations, and metrics so they know what success looks like and they know how they will grow

B. Team members are empowered and given latitude and tools to do their job well

C. Regular inspections and feedback improve team member performance

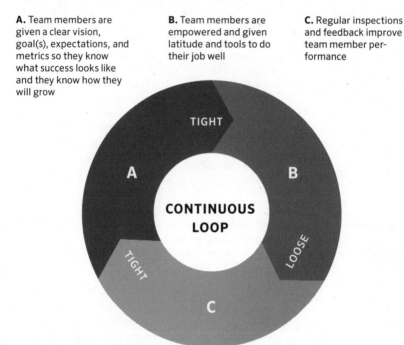

Let's look at what each of these terms means in more detail.

A. Tight: Make sure that all employees have set clear goals for themselves and have declared their career aspirations. In a "tight" setting, employees understand the expectations leaders have of them and the role they play in helping the firm achieve its goals.

This clarity will ensure that employees begin to feel a sense of accountability. It is key that you link your employees' aspirations to the objectives of the organization and team. If you disconnect the employee's growth and career progress from what you need them to do for the organization, then they will never feel that acute sense of accountability.

In this way, we make the accountability personal. We can take this a step further, as most organizations do, by making sure employees have clear metrics, such as key performance indicators (KPIs). These metrics need to be specific, measurable, and time-bound. Essentially, each employee is "tight" on what success looks like in their role.

B. Loose: Let the employees get on with it. Empower them. Don't insist on doing it your way. Admittedly, this method requires quite a bit of bravery and trust on the part of the leader. In his book *Drive*, Daniel Pink summarizes employee engagement research into three main drivers: mastery, purpose, and autonomy.[6] The "loose" part is giving the employee autonomy.

We're all built with an inner drive. Edward L. Deci and his colleague Richard Ryan have explored the nature of self-determination theory, a theory of motivation that takes into account people's psychological needs. They revealed in a study of workers at an investment bank that when managers offered autonomy support, employees reported higher job satisfaction and there was better overall job performance.[7]

Autonomy support means helping employees progress by giving them choice about how to do things as well as encouragement. Workplaces can support autonomy by giving employees control over various aspects of their work—like deciding what to work on or when to do it. Virgin is one of the world leaders in terms of creating autonomy. As Richard Branson says, "We give our people real autonomy. We encourage employees to take advantage of flexible work hours. They can opt for alternative schedules, to work from home, or to work from one of our other offices."[8] The idea is that if you are "tight" with your expectations in A, and employees understand what's in it for them, then autonomy in B becomes so much easier because they have clear expectations and they're motivated. They know working hard will help them become more successful too.

C. *Tight*: Inspect what you expect. Check in with employees frequently. An important part of the final "tight" is providing coaching or feedback to individual employees to help them improve their performance and reach their goals.

If you are "tight" with your expectations and then empower your employees ("loose"), but you do not follow up to provide feedback and allow them to perform even better (the "tight" in C), then they will start to lose accountability. When a leader consistently turns up to observe what the employee is doing and provides feedback, so they can make progress toward goals, then the employee will own the outcomes even more.

When no one turns up to give high-quality feedback in C and simply relies on the employee performing at the level they laid out in the first "tight" in A, employees lose motivation and a sense of ownership. I will tackle this issue in great detail in the final part of the book—endurance. At this point, it's important to know that we must build in continual high-quality feedback to teams and employees, so that they always feel like they are developing their ability to achieve the goals they helped set in the first "tight."

Continuous loop: In this respect, the final "tight" in C allows us to provide a continuous feedback loop into the first "tight" in A. This loop is one of continually coaching and providing high-quality feedback, so they are even clearer (tighter) on what is expected of them and how they can excel. In this way, the tight-loose-tight model is self-reinforcing.

CASE STUDY: Commonwealth Bank of Australia

COMMONWEALTH BANK IS a fantastic example of both executing at the service system level and using a tight-loose-tight model.

In 2007, the Commonwealth Bank of Australia was the worst out of the country's five major banks in terms of delivering service. Now they have been the best bank in Australia since 2012—five years in a row![9]

The journey to number one consists of two parts—designing the service system and executing the service system. This case study focuses on the design of the service system.

Designing a compelling service vision

The first step in redesigning Commonwealth Bank's service approach was to create a service vision that is clear, compelling, and memorable. This service vision would propel us forward and create excitement about our goals. The vision we created was this: To be the finest financial services organization in Australia through excelling in customer service and to be number one out of the major banks by June 30, 2010.

The vision turned out to powerful for three reasons.

First, it was succinct and clear. No ambiguity, no smoke and mirrors. Simplicity. We wanted to be the best through service. Not the best out of *all* the banks in Australia (not small local banks, for example) but the major five banks (there are now four, after two merged), which we could easily track against.

Second, we wanted to *excel* in service. While many service visions have throwaway words, we chose every word carefully. Recall in the last chapter, the discovery that excelling in service (scoring nine or ten out of ten) makes an incredible impact over good service (sevens or eights). We knew this and it was what we shot for—excellent customer feedback in all the measures that we tracked. In every survey we conducted (in call centres, branches, and private banks, with salespeople and through internal service surveys), we tracked and rewarded only for nines and tens. In this way, we zeroed in on excellent service.

Third, and this bit I insisted on, we put a timeframe on it: number one by June 30, 2010. You cannot weasel out of a clear deadline that is communicated in every possible way. Importantly, this created a sense of urgency. The clock was now ticking—we had three years to do this or we would lose credibility with all employees who would see this as an empty goal. Imagine the procrastination that would have occurred without a deadline. As it turned out, adding this date created momentum in ways we never imagined.

Creating scorecards that link to the vision

With this vision and strategy in place, we created service scorecards for all areas based on customer data—business banking, retail banking, insurance, and wealth management. These customer scorecards were broken down into the 3RS—reliability measures, responsiveness measures, and relationship measures. Using the framework of the 3RS enabled us to make execution easy to understand and to connect with how we asked employees to deliver service.

Each measure was then given a traffic-light colour by the team who collected the metrics. Red indicated we were a long way from the target. Amber showed we were close to the target. Green meant that measure was met or exceeded (for example, if 80 percent of home loan applications were completed within our assigned timeframe).

These customer scorecards were then driven down to the areas of the bank that "owned" that measure. A VP's name was directly assigned to each measure, and they then created their own scorecards with lead measures to push the rolled-up scorecard forward.

Fixing broken processes

Next, these scorecards, with the assistance of the process excellence area of the bank (i.e., Lean Six Sigma types), were linked to the process improvements occurring across the bank. To help with this process, a CEO customer service forum was created where, once a month, all heads of the respective areas of the bank (HR and marketing, sales and service, IT, CEO, all business unit areas, and me as general manager of customer satisfaction) made decisions based on the scorecard.

Each business unit head went through their scorecard in the meeting. We glossed over measures that were green to focus on ambers and reds in detail—particularly if they were reliability measures. Given the status of the people in the room, process investment decisions in many cases could be made there. We put a ninety-day window on improving these processes; if no real change had occurred after ninety days, we would escalate a review of this process.

Process reviews were continuous. It was a great way to pay attention to a broken process and put it in the spotlight. It also ensured these processes were important to the customer, rather than focusing on those with little impact on the customer experience. Finally, the CEO customer service forum (run by the CEO, which gave it integrity) was a very useful way to hold each business unit of the bank accountable for their scorecard. Remember, they had to talk through the scorecard with the CEO present as well as their peers—there is no escaping from the numbers!

Implementing HR policies and practices

Finally, Commonwealth Bank of Australia did a fantastic job linking the service strategy, customer scorecards, and process improvements to important HR policies and practices.

One really important way this occurred was when 40 percent of everyone's discretionary bonus was tied to customer satisfaction: the CEO, everyone in IT, HR, all front-liners, all team leaders, all managers, including me—everyone. Before this, it varied between 0 and 20 percent. If you want to excel in customer satisfaction but you are rewarding sales or efficiency measures instead, this sends out a very strong (and wrong) message.

For many areas of the bank, we made sales and service worth the same (40 percent each)—we needed to sell, but not if it meant sacrificing service. There are no silver bullets when delivering great service and designing a strong service system, but assigning the same value to sales and service was one of the most powerful things we did.

We also connected the service system with HR policies and practices through hiring and onboarding. Employees were hired based on their potential to grow into service superstars. We were much more focused on new hires' willingness to be coached (see chapter 8 for more on coaching for service) than on their previous work experience. Orientations were also designed around the 3Rs. New employees were shown the key customer metrics they would be evaluated on and how they could influence these lead measures to drive higher levels of service.

Living the system

This system was kept alive every week through customer feedback—tied to the 40 percent bonus for reaching service levels—which was passed on to every branch, call centre team, and salesperson every Friday afternoon. This led to the "Friday feeling," an anxious wait as to whether you had hit your service targets or not. It kept the momentum going—whether your targets were on track or not—and gave detailed feedback that all teams, even back-office teams, could use to guide their work.

Finally, each team across the bank had a twice-weekly service and sales meeting on Monday mornings and Friday afternoons (which was like an after-action review) to discuss ways to improve on service and sales. Each Monday morning, a different topic was discussed and a "big five" was created: the team came up with five new ideas to implement each week. On Fridays, we would discuss how well these five new ideas had worked.

Overall, this service system turned out to be robust. There is no doubt that integrating all of the pieces of the puzzle and subsequently designing each element was the foundation for reaching and staying at number one.

Over the past ten years, since the Commonwealth Bank started this journey, their shares have gone up 40 percent more than the next best major bank in Australia—and in some cases, 90 percent more. That's because the Commonwealth Bank has built an organization to last, out-rivalling everyone through enduring service.

Recap

It takes a lot of work to knock down a strong service system. Without this system, your service plans can disappear almost overnight with a budgeting crisis, new leadership, acquisition, or any other tornado that hits. A house of cards is easily blown over.

Employees who feel accountable and own the quality of their work turn every service encounter into gold. The service system provides that alchemy.

FAME PART 3
MOMENTS OF POWER

F RAMEWORKS AND ACCOUNTABILITY set the stage for employees to deliver outstanding service. However, even with frameworks in place and employees feeling accountable, they can fall down in a service interaction. If employees do not know how identify the "moments of power" that make a difference, then they will never maximize the potential of the customer interaction. By making the most of these moments, employees have a better chance of delivering service that stands out from the competition.

I have boiled down the implementation of great service into four moments of power. Together, these four moments enable you to execute the service system, in particular the 3Rs. As we go through these moments, I will identify what it is about each of them that makes a difference. By understanding these moments and delivering on them when they arise, organizations increase the probability that customers will return, refer, and recommend.

Just like the rest of this book, these moments are rooted in science. I didn't come up with these by sitting in a comfortable armchair, with a clawing cat on my lap, pondering the most important moments in service. No! I came up with these through extensive research on social psychology, behavioural science, psychology, and neuroscience. The research points to four moments that can make a difference from the customer's point of view:

1. **Power of Context:** What you do before you deliver service is as important as the service you deliver. This moment of power is all about creating a strong service culture within your team, adopting a growth mindset,[1] and framing information and situations for the customer to guide their behaviour. We can change someone's experience by simply restructuring what they think, feel, or see beforehand.

2. **Power of Expertise:** The moment when a customer realizes they are talking to an employee who is an expert, who owns the customer experience, and who is always reliable is the most influential moment in service. Expertise demonstrates reliability and responsiveness, the most important of the 3Rs. This moment of power is about how to develop expertise in employees and how to continually demonstrate expertise in the customer's eyes.

3. **Power of Relationships:** This moment of power is about how to personalize the experience, how to "go first"—doing things for the customer that are unexpected and meaningful—how to deepen the relationship with the customer, and how to genuinely compliment the customer. It also captures the importance of "liking the one that you are with": having a positive attitude toward the customer before they walk through the door and maintaining that positive attitude.

4. **Power of Problem Handling:** Effectively handling customer problems can change your relationship with them in a heartbeat. When you handle a problem well, the customer may be even more loyal than before the problem. If you handle it badly, then you have failed twice. This moment of power explores the impact of problem handling and how to handle customer problems successfully.

In combination, and when paired with the right frameworks and systems (the F and A of parts one and two), these four moments of power will help you continually deliver great service.

Let's have a close look at these moments of power.

4

Power of Context

"**W**HY DID YOU choose Kiwi Experience?" Winton asked Rory, as the Interislander ferry pulled away from the Wellington harbour on its three-and-a-half-hour trip to Picton in the South Island.

"I never really planned to, before I left Scotland. I'd always planned to hire a campervan," replied Rory.

"So, what made you change your mind then?" asked Winton.

"I kept hearing of KE when I was travelling around Australia. Every time I stopped at a backpackers', I'd meet at least one person who would have a KE story to tell. I was swayed by the crowd, I think. When I came to New Zealand, KE did a presentation at the backpackers' where I was staying and that really did it for me."

Many service organizations can rely on repeat purchases to maintain and enhance their profitability. Not KE, however. It is very unusual for passengers to travel on KE twice. The company relies on new customers for virtually all of their sales. Social proof (evidence that if others are doing it, then it must be the right behaviour) is critical for KE.

Kiwi Experience promotes heavily in its target market and, wherever possible, attempts to stimulate word-of-mouth. Research shows that 75 percent of customers have heard of KE before they enter New Zealand, assisting in sales as customers are familiar with the service before they purchase it. Kiwi Experience does two other things to harness the crowd beyond delivering a great experience to every passenger while they are on the bus.

First, KE expertly uses social media to influence customers to choose KE before they land in New Zealand. Encouraging KE passengers to share images of the incredible scenery they are seeing in the moment works incredibly well. The implied message is simple: "Other passengers are seeing and doing this right now; wouldn't you like to experience this as well?" Check out the #KiwiExperience photos on Instagram.

Second, once the backpackers are in the country, KE deploys "street fighters": backpackers who hand out brochures at railway terminals, bus stations, and so on throughout the "gateway" sites of Auckland and Christchurch. They also spread the word at backpacker hostels. Kiwi Experience likes using backpackers who have been on the bus as they are informed, motivated, and credible communicators who can sell the KE service better than anyone else. Kiwi Experience, it seems, really does fight for every customer they get by using the power of the crowd.

The insight here is that the employees at KE are social psychology experts. They know that human behaviour is driven by the environment that surrounds us; in this case, the best form of promotion is from backpackers who are like the potential customer. Similarity is a huge driver in social proof—we follow others *like* us.

Understanding the context in which your customers and employees reside and managing it to your fullest advantage is a key tenet of service excellence.

Do men have only two emotions?

Human behaviour is sensitive and strongly influenced by its surroundings—in fact, more so than we've ever realized. Before we talk about the power of context, one of the moments of power mentioned above, I would like to give you a little quiz. What is the golden rule of social psychology?

a. In a contest between an individual's personality and the situation you put them in, the individual's personality is generally a better indicator of their future behaviour.
b. People follow others in every situation.
c. In a contest between an individual's personality and the situation you put them in, the situation is generally a better predictor of their future behaviour.
d. Men have only two emotions.

The correct answer is D! No, not really, it's C.

The golden rule, according to social psychologists, lies in the competition between the context in which you put someone and their individual personality.[1] Context—not their individual personality—is most likely to drive their behaviour. Simply put, if you have a negative environment, then people will behave destructively; if you create an encouraging environment, then they'll behave positively. You can shape that context for the customer and the employee.

For example, the research indicates that if you place someone who is fantastic at delivering service on a team that is more focused on themselves than being responsive to customers, the new employee will adapt their behaviour to the team's behaviour. They will slowly regress to the team's standards and deliver less than stellar service. Conversely, take someone who's never delivered great service in their life and put them in a team that excels at looking after the customer. The employee will adapt their behaviour to the team and deliver ever-increasing service, as the culture dictates. We must always think about how we can create the best possible context for both the employees who deliver service and the customers who receive service.

A good example of shaping context—in this case, the physical context—is supermarkets. Years have been spent researching the optimal physical environment in which customers are most likely to purchase products—from the smell to the height of the ceiling, the width of the aisles, and even down to the product placement. The random tub of ice cream you bought yesterday was likely because of the man dressed like a cow walking around the supermarket who subliminally changed your purchasing habits.

This chapter zeroes in on three particular paths to help you manage the context in your favour:

1. **Culture:** The stronger the service culture inside your organization, the likelier that customers will receive great service.

2. **Growth mindset:** Only employees and leaders with a growth mindset will be able to fulfill their potential in delivering great service. People with this mindset see effort, coaching, feedback, and learning goals as the path to mastery.

3. **Framing:** How you frame information and requests *before* the customers receive service will dramatically impact the service and the choices they make when they receive service.

Path 1: Culture

Every organization has its own culture, whether intentionally created or not. Are you willing to shape a more dynamic service culture? Before a customer walks through the door, you can create a positive work environment—one where everyone wants to and knows how to serve the customer.

Here are the four characteristics that organizations need in order to create a strong service culture. As with the disciplines in chapter 3, if you take one of these characteristics away, then you're less likely to have a strong service culture. All of these cultural traits are important.

Alignment

Alignment happens when everyone is drawn to the same sense of purpose—they understand the service vision and goals of the organization and team they are working in, and they are excited by that sense of purpose. When everyone is pushing against each other and no one has a true sense of where their team or the organization is going, they won't create a healthy service culture. A sense of alignment across the organization is a strong cultural trait, and a critical one.

This alignment applies to the back office as well as the front office. So often the back office is disengaged in executing on the service vision, but their buy-in causes the whole organization to move forward much more effectively.

The Whistler Blackcomb case study later in this chapter demonstrates that one of the most potent things they did was to get buy-in from everyone in the organization to raise the bar on customer service.

Behavioural framework

Every organization I've worked with that has built service FAME has a tight behavioural framework. This framework is agreed upon across the organization and identifies desirable behaviours for all employees to display with the customer and each other. Ensuring that people understand and have agreed to exactly what they should be doing gives you a lot more leverage in training, coaching, and receiving feedback on those particular behaviours.

When you don't have a behavioural framework or values, then people adopt whatever behaviours they think are right. In the best-case scenario, there will be inconsistency. Having a tight behavioural framework encourages everyone to push in the same direction, and it creates replicable, memorable experiences across the organization much faster.

The 3Rs of reliability (essentially fulfilling customer needs), responsiveness (making it easy and efficient to do business together), and relationships (connecting with customers) is a great example of a behavioural framework.

If you'll recall, Tony Hsieh, CEO of Zappos, said that it doesn't matter what your values are, just that you commit to them and they become a habit. And this is a key point: without a strong behavioural framework, employees will likely lack a true sense of how they should behave with each other and with the customer, which could hold the organization back.

Servant leaders

In a service context, leaders continually reinforce the importance of paying attention to service by serving people inside the organization—particularly those they're leading.

Robert Greenleaf, a researcher who founded the modern servant leadership movement and the Greenleaf Center for Servant Leadership, has done remarkable research on servant leadership. Greenleaf states servant leaders, unlike traditional leaders, primarily focus on the growth and well-being of people.[2] When people grow and achieve their goals in the workplace, they simultaneously provide customers with exceptional service. Servant leaders pass off some of their power onto employees by putting employees' needs first and helping them develop and perform at a higher level.

As Greenleaf asserts, "The difference manifests itself in the care taken by the servant—first to make sure other people's highest priority needs are being served. The best test, and difficult to administer, is: Do those served grow as persons? Do they, while being served, become healthier, wiser, freer, more autonomous, more likely themselves to become servants?"[3]

When servant leaders pass this test, they are creating the conditions for a very strong service culture. Compare this to leaders who spend most of their time pushing themselves forward, making little time to grow their team. Chapter 8 explores in more depth the role of servant leaders in coaching employees to grow their service skills.

Customer fixation

One recurring theme you see across the case studies in this book, from Kiwi Experience, Amazon, and Whistler Blackcomb to the Commonwealth Bank and Pan Pacific Hotels, is their fixation on customers as a deep cultural trait. But aren't all organizations fixated with customers? Sadly, no. Shouldn't you develop customer fixation if you want to build your service FAME? Yes!

To fixate on customers means to think very deeply about them, to create commitments to ensure you never forget what they need from you, and to use this fixation as the constant cornerstone of your approach. Most companies think *about* customers, but they don't think *like* them. And that is a crucial difference.

The first step in being fixated with customers is to remove your fixation with competitors. As we will see in the case study in the next chapter, from very early on, Amazon focused on customers. As Jeff Bezos, Amazon's CEO, states, "We're not competitor obsessed, we're customer obsessed. We start with what the customer needs and we work backwards."[4]

A customer fixation means, for example, continuously developing deep insights into what customers like, love, and dream about. You won't get this information through customer surveys, but from thinking like them, talking to them, and observing them—essentially whatever you need to do to truly understand them. It also means continuously innovating on their behalf, always thinking of better ways of serving and redesigning processes to make it easier for them—even when customers haven't said one bad thing about that process. Finally, it also means sacrificing short-term profitability for long-term value. You must be willing to make mistakes, reverse decisions, and apologize when things go wrong. You must align your reward systems to be consistent a long-term value focus too.

This customer fixation has much to do with the first cultural trait of alignment: we will only make progress when all leaders agree with the idea that customers must always be at the centre of everything we do.

CASE STUDY: Whistler Blackcomb— Creating a stronger service culture

IN 2015, MIRIAM MacDonald, the newly appointed head of the Whistler Blackcomb Service Project for the more than 4,000 staff, was concerned about how to embed the new Whistler Experience program—built on the moments of power and the 3Rs—without losing any momentum. After all, Whistler Blackcomb (WB) was already the number one ski resort in North America, as voted by *Ski Magazine* readers. The stakes were extremely high.

The first thing MacDonald did was meet the manager of employee experience and the general managers for sales, who had managed the trial program the season before with great success. With their insights and suggestions, she put together a service team of twelve managers from across WB, each representing a division, and created a project timeline for the year with an approved budget. Both front- and back-of-house teams were involved. For the first year, WB focused on the 3RS and the first two moments of power: power of expertise and power of relationships. MacDonald is also part of the Whistler Chamber of Commerce service committee. Working with that team, MacDonald shared successes and challenges at WB.

Whistler Blackcomb sent materials to each service team member and asked them to customize them for their departments. Service team members also shared information and training plans amongst themselves.

Whistler Blackcomb then offered customized training to 200 staff in their own fall training, beyond the public workshops offered as part of the Whistler Experience. The trainees were a cross-section of supervisors and managers, and it was a great way to get everyone on the same page. MacDonald had posters designed and created for all back-of-house staff areas. They introduced this new service program in the first-season staff orientation sessions and return season staff sessions, outlining why they believed it would be more effective, useful, and positive for both employees and guests.

This behavioural framework was then used by every team across WB on a regular basis. Whenever there was a team meeting, the 3RS framework was used to talk about key service concepts and how each team could bring them alive in their area every day, providing a focus on service.

Alignment

Probably the greatest success was getting all areas of WB to buy in to the program; as MacDonald said, "There was a strong culture of service before, especially among front-line employees. This program broadened the focus to *all* divisions. The awareness of service belonging to everyone, not just front-facing staff, was one of the main points I spoke to and focused on."

This alignment offered a new sense of purpose and vision. The service team and MacDonald met each month for two years to execute the 3Rs and other aspects of great service (for example, see handling problems in chapter 7). MacDonald created an agenda for each monthly meeting with updates on their current service score rankings, goals, and guest comments about WB's staff. Each team discussed what was working and what was not in their areas. They also brainstormed and shared recognition ideas that worked with their teams.

This new approach created a stronger service culture across the whole company, not just front-of-house. Also, by sharing their experiences with other Whistler businesses at Whistler Chamber of Commerce meetings, WB built a sense of community within the village.

Servant leaders

Servant leaders, like MacDonald, focus on the needs of others, especially team members, above their own. Leaders at WB acknowledge other employees' perspectives, give them the support they need to complete their work (hence their new focus on coaching) and achieve personal goals, involve them in decisions where appropriate, and build a strong sense of community. These changes led to higher engagement at Whistler Blackcomb, more psychological safety, and stronger relationships with team members and other stakeholders.

WB usually had two profound "dips" in service scores over a ski season (looking at previous ski season data), but rather than beat employees over the head with the importance of delivering service consistently over the whole twenty weeks, they took another approach. In their first year, MacDonald identified some later weeks in the spring season and focused her efforts to drive change then. As MacDonald states, "We created a voucher package for each manager and senior leader (ninety of them) to carry with them and recognize great work within their teams and among other WB divisions. These vouchers were good for a snack or beverage. The direction we gave to each leader was to be out and about with your teams, actively recognizing all staff."

Whistler Blackcomb succeeded in maintaining consistent scores and avoiding the service dip. For the second year, they addressed the other "dip" area—the early season, roughly around the third week of operations. Again, applying the same strategy as they had for spring, vouchers were created and distributed to all leaders with the same message. In this way, WB successfully maintained their early season scores and avoided the dip. The team at WB used leadership to generate engagement rather than flexing their punitive muscle.

Servant leaders recognize employees meaningfully

Another important characteristic of a servant leader is the way they recognize employees who are doing a great job. Whenever you celebrate outstanding service, you put the employees forward rather than the leaders. Whistler Blackcomb took a unique approach with the roll-out of the new program.

MacDonald described this new approach: "I didn't want to take from the many recognition programs we currently have in place that are successful, so I created a new event to focus just on celebrating service. I created the 3RS' Service Winners Lunch."

To be nominated for this monthly lunch in one of the on-hill fine-dining restaurants, peers, supervisors, or a manager had to fill out a ballot online. These votes went to the service team and were taken to the divisional managers' meetings to choose a winner. Larger divisions got to choose two or three winners each month. MacDonald then sent out individual invites to the lunch.

A member of the senior leadership team attended and everyone was paid for the afternoon. Their photos were featured in the WB staff newsletter each month.

Results

Given that WB was already the number one ski resort in North America, the improvements in service scores have been noteworthy. Any improvement, when you are the best already, is excellent news and shows a growth mindset in action. They achieved their best score ever in the 2016–17 season with over 80 percent for employee service for the first time. This is a 7 percent improvement in four years.

The future

MacDonald has formulated two ideas to improve. Some divisions (snow-making, for example) found the training schedule in the fall clashed with their huge volume of work at that time. MacDonald wants to get to these divisions in the future.

Also, some parts of WB had been proactive and created customized courses, such as for private ski instructors. These have been really effective, more so than the regular service training for WB as a whole. Budget allowing, MacDonald wanted to offer department-specific training, so WB could really drill down in each division.

This relentless focus on continuously improving service over the long haul sums up the customer fixation of MacDonald and WB. You can never stand still with your service culture because to stay at number one, you have to be as hungry as if you were number two. That hunger is what WB shows through their approach. Every. Single. Day.

Path 2: Growth mindset

This section is based on Carol Dweck's incredible work, which has been adopted by many organizations worldwide. Dweck found that what drives success in people is not their innate ability, but what they *believe* it can be developed into.[5]

She discovered that people in most areas of life have either a "fixed mindset" or a "growth mindset." A fixed mindset holds the belief that traits such as intelligence and personality cannot be changed (although people with a fixed mindset tend to believe people still have the ability to learn new things). Consequently, someone with a fixed mindset tends to process and understand a person's behaviour or outcomes in terms of their fixed traits.

People with a "growth mindset" believe traits can be cultivated and changed, and they have the potential to become more intelligent through effort. Dweck and colleagues found that having a growth mindset—conceiving of personal attributes as dynamic, malleable qualities—may diminish the importance of traits in understanding behaviour, while focusing more intently on specific factors such as needs and goals that support behaviour and outcome.[6]

Probably the biggest difference between people with fixed and growth mindsets is how they see effort. Fixed mindset people see effort as a sign of low intelligence—effort is for those who don't have the ability. As Dweck contends, "People with a growth mindset believe something very different. For them, even geniuses have to work hard for their achievements. Growth mindset people may appreciate endowment, but they admire effort, for no matter what your abilities, effort is what ignites the ability and turns it into accomplishment."[7]

Fixed mindset people see high effort as a big risk because if they try and fail, they are left without any excuses. However, growth mindset people see low effort as the big risk: having a goal but doing nothing about it is the big risk.

I'm a strong advocate for bringing the idea of these mindsets into organizations, particularly to help create the correct approach in serving the customer. In terms of service, employees with a fixed mindset rely on their natural talents to serve a customer; they are less likely to put in the effort to get better at service (by attending training sessions, for example, or practicing service skills), because they don't believe it will make a big difference. Growth mindset people want to learn and grow, and they want to take on challenges posed by leaders. They see effort as the path to mastery. They simply know they're unlikely to get better at serving customers unless they practice news skills and work hard at their expertise.

Resilience

Dweck and her colleagues also found a distinct difference in how people with a fixed mindset handle setbacks, as opposed to people with a growth mindset.[8] People with fixed mindsets were found to be more likely to react to a failure by questioning and doubting their ability. Furthermore, they were more likely to adopt a passive outlook in terms of successfully accomplishing similar tasks in the future. Conversely, people with a growth mindset tended to focus more on behavioural factors in an attempt to identify reasons why they did not rise to the challenge. They then develop a new strategy aimed at improving their abilities as they continue to work toward mastery.

In short, fixed mindset people lack resilience and grit and are more likely to give up in the face of setbacks. They also are more likely to avoid challenges, simply because they are afraid to fail. Growth mindset people see failure as the path to mastery and, because of this, they develop resilience and grit, learning to pick themselves up and face the next challenge. Resilience and grit are necessary for building expertise, which is the most important factor of service excellence, as we will see later.

Fixed mindset employees see challenging customers and situations as simply annoying and want the problem to go away as quickly as possible. Growth mindset employees see challenging customers and situations as a chance to develop grit—winning over the toughest of customers. When things don't go according to plan, they know this experience will help them be better next time.

Feedback

Fixed mindset people seek feedback, particularly negative feedback, as something that defines them. They will likely ignore, or at least discount, the feedback, given that they believe talent is the main driver of success. People with a growth mindset demand feedback, so they can grow and move forward on the road to mastery.

In short, people with a growth mindset put feedback to work. In a neuroscience study conducted at Columbia University, the researchers monitored students' brain activity while they responded to questions and then received feedback on their answers. After the feedback session, the students were given an unexpected retest that included all of the questions they answered inaccurately the first time.[9] Students who held a growth mindset got more answers right on the surprise retest, suggesting they'd made better use of the feedback. Evidence from brain-activation monitors showed that people with growth mindsets and people with fixed mindsets actually process feedback information differently, as related by cognitive psychologist Scott Barry Kaufman in his book *Ungifted*.[10]

Thus, employees with a growth mindset will seek feedback from servant leaders in order to become better at delivering service, while employees with a fixed mindset are less likely to use feedback to raise their performance. A refusal to improve their skills will, of course, hold them and the organization back in delivering service excellence.

How to move from a fixed to a growth mindset

There are many ways to help someone move from a fixed mindset to a growth mindset. The first step is to teach people about the different mindsets—once people understand that they may have a fixed mindset, they are more likely to try to change it. Another fantastic way of getting someone into a growth mindset, as we will see in chapter 8, is coaching. When you coach someone, you are continually getting the coachee to push themselves out of their comfort zone and to see the possibilities that come from effort, feedback, and practice. Finally, using growth-mindset language is particularly powerful. Use the word "yet" when you haven't mastered something; when you fail, remind yourself that "fail" simply means *first attempt in learning*.

Path 3: Framing

What you do *before* the customer turns up may be just as important as the service you provide when they are there. The way in which you frame information and requests can make such a difference, and it is all underpinned by how our brain works.

Our brain: systems 1 and 2

In his book *Thinking, Fast and Slow*, Daniel Kahneman shows us that we comprehend the world in two radically opposed ways, employing two fundamentally different modes of thought: system 1 and system 2.[11]

System 1 is fast; it's intuitive, associative, metaphorical, automatic, impressionistic, and it can't be switched off. Its operations involve no sense of intentional control, but it's the "secret author of many of the choices and judgments you make."[12]

System 2 is slow, deliberate, and effortful. Its operations require attention. System 2 takes over, rather unwillingly, when things get difficult. But system 2 is not in charge; system 1 is. System 2 is sluggish and tires easily (a process called ego depletion), so it usually accepts what system 1 tells it. It's often right to do so, because system 1 is, for the most part, good at what it does; it's highly sensitive to subtle environmental cues, signs of danger, and so on. It does, however, pay a high price for speed.[13]

A great example of system 1 comes from a study of hundreds of customers who received gift certificates worth six dollars, good for a coffee and cake at a local high-quality bakery.[14] Half of the group received a voucher that would expire in twenty-one days and the other half had vouchers that were good for sixty days. Before they gave the vouchers out to anyone, the researchers asked a preliminary group of people if they'd prefer the sixty-day or the twenty-one-day and, of course, every single one of them said they would choose the sixty-day. When they asked people if they'd actually use them, 68 percent of the sixty-day group said, "Yes, I will use this voucher." However, only 50 percent of the twenty-one-day group said, "Yes, I would use this voucher."

After sixty days, they collected the used vouchers from the bakery. Which group do you think used the voucher more? Only 6 percent of the sixty-day group used the voucher, whereas 32 percent of the twenty-one-day group did.[15] Three incredible findings from this research highlight system 1:

1. The sixty-day voucher was most popular, yet it was a disadvantage for the people who took it. You likely knew that the sixty-day voucher is less likely to be used than the twenty-one-day, but we would all still choose the sixty-day because two months gives us more time to redeem it. Choosing an option that is likely bad for us is a great example of system 1 behaviour.
2. Another system 1 characteristic is that we are bad at predicting our own behaviour—in this case, 68 percent of this sixty-day group said they would use it and only a tiny proportion (6 percent) did.
3. The recipients with a tighter deadline of three weeks used the voucher. System 1 creates a sense of urgency.

Another remarkable study, concerning the physical environment, was published in the journal *Science*.[16] Researchers created an alleyway, peppered with graffiti and litter, next to a shopping centre where people always parked their bikes. Over a number of weeks, the researchers attached an advert for a fictional store to the handlebars of these bikes. The cyclists couldn't ride their bikes away until they took this advertisement off because it was in the way. The researchers recorded the data and then they cleaned the alleyway up, painted it, made it clean, and did the same experiment again. When the alleyway was covered in graffiti, 69 percent of people took the advert that was on the bike and threw it on the ground, but when it was a clean alleyway, only 33 percent of people tossed it on the ground.

Notice the dramatic change in human behaviour just by changing what they saw beforehand.

System 1 reacts to the context, which is especially important in terms of customer behaviour. What often looks like a customer issue is actually a context issue, so by managing the context and changing the environment, you can change people's behaviour.

Contrast effect

A big part of framing is also what researchers call the "contrast effect"— when we see two different things in a sequence, we tend to see the second one as more different from the first than if we'd seen it in isolation. It's called perceptual contrast, which means the background established before making a request may be more important than the request itself. It's a great example of system 1 in action.

The principle here is a psychological phenomenon known as anchoring. Anchoring describes cases in which a person uses a specific target number or value as a starting point, known as an anchor, and subsequently adjusts that information until an acceptable value is reached over time. Often, those adjustments are inadequate and remain too close to the original anchor. Anchor values can be self-generated, the output of a pricing model or forecasting tool, or suggested by an outside individual like a business. Anchoring allows you to highlight the best choice for your customers and, for you, gives it the shine it deserves.

I was at a social psychology conference recently when one of the attendees stood up and told a story about the power of framing prices in the right way using anchoring and heuristics. The speaker owned forty dentist offices across the U.S. and was having difficulty selling his best-quality dentures (roughly US$8,000). He was frustrated because these dentures were clearly in the customer's best interest, as they were much higher quality and would last a lot longer than the cheapest pair. He contacted a retailing consultant to help him understand why people were not buying the dentures that gave them the highest-quality teeth and best smile. In twenty of the dentist offices, they continued selling the dentures in the same way they always had: the dentist first outlined the entry-level dentures (roughly $2,000), then next best dentures ($4,000), then second-best dentures ($6,000), and finally the premium model ($8,000). In the other twenty offices, they reversed the order and started with the best-quality dentures, working their way down to the entry-level dentures.

When the dentist started with $2,000 dentures, the $8,000 ones seemed incredibly expensive for most people, and so the most popular were the compromise choice at $4,000. These were better quality than entry level but a lot less than the two higher-priced dentures they heard about next. When the pitch order changed, however, the $6,000 became the most popular because the anchoring point became the $8,000 set, which the patient heard explained first. Now the $4,000 dentures seemed completely inferior. They achieved an average 50–60 percent increase in revenue by just changing the order in which they listed and described products for their customers.

Very few businesses know this. Look at a restaurant's wine list: it almost always goes from the cheapest to the most expensive. Try getting a restaurant patron to buy a hundred-dollar bottle of wine if the first one they see is only thirty dollars. I'm not suggesting restaurant owners should list them from the most expensive to the cheapest (although, I did see a restaurant in Montréal do this once), but what I do know is that starting with the cheapest is a bad idea (especially given that the thirty-dollar wine may not provide the customers with the best experience). Restaurants could, for example, list the wines in order of vintage instead of by price.

Power of social proof

Finally, a very important part of framing is how you highlight what other customers are doing. A great example of the power of the crowd is seen in an experiment on towels. I love towels—they are the best invention of all time. Some people say the motorcar is the best invention, but look how the motorcar has polluted the world. Some say the internet was the best invention ever, but look at how much Facebook has ruined us—"Look at our friends, their lives are way better than ours, they are off to the moon ... again."[17] Think about it, if you came out of the shower and the towel hadn't been invented, how would you dry yourself? You might think you just have to shake yourself dry, but that would be really uncomfortable for everyone. Anyway, I particularly love thick and fluffy towels, which you tend to find in hotels. In fact, they're so thick and fluffy I can hardly close my suitcase when I pack to leave...[18]

So, on the subject of towels, my favourite experiment ever was done in an Arizona hotel, where they created a new method of reusing towels to help save the environment.[19] These clever experimenters posted three different signs in hotel-room bathrooms. Some rooms had a standard sign asking guests to reuse towels in order to be environmentally friendly. Other rooms had signs stating, "Almost 75 percent of guests who are asked to participate in our new resource savings program help by using their towels more than once. You can join your fellow guests." They're saying please don't be a jerk—join the towel reusers and be part of the crowd. Now, interestingly, they came up with a third sign that read, "Almost 75 percent of guests who stay in this room ... " and they included the room number (say, 617)—which is a little bit creepy if you ask me, because you'll be thinking, "Am I reusing someone else's towel?"

With just the environmental-focused sign, only 35 percent of people reused a towel on the second night (they only tested on the second night, not the third, fourth, and so on). When it was "75 percent of guests in this hotel reuse ... ," it was 44 percent of people—a 9 percent increase in usage. When it was "in this room," it went up 14 percent to 49 percent. Researchers call this a "provincial social norm" focus—in other words, the more real you make it, the more likely others will follow it.

Social norms are one of the most powerful ways to frame a request, as it highlights what other customers are doing. What you need to remember is customers *want* to know what other customers are doing. If many other customers are doing something, then customers think, "I should do it too." This is another great example of system 1—the magnetism of the crowd.

Just think of how Amazon uses social proof. From endless product reviews, highlighting what other customers do after browsing the item you are looking at (e.g., what other products they frequently buy with your item) to revealing the most popular books, watches, hats, and so on, their use of the power of the crowd is extensive. And if Amazon, the most successful retailer on the planet, is using it, shouldn't you?

Recap

The power of context allows us to prepare for memorable service encounters by changing what the customer sees beforehand. With a strong customer-first culture, we are building a strong service environment *before* the customer does business with us.

By having an organization that focuses on the growth mindset, employees will develop their service abilities all the time, rather than relying on their natural-born abilities.

Finally, by understanding how to frame information and requests in the right way, *before* we serve the customer, we can help customers make their best decisions. In particular, focus on the contrast effect and social norms as effective ways of managing the context.

RANDOM STORY:
The Power of Losing

ONE AREA OF the power of context I did not cover is prospect the-ory, the discovery of which won Daniel Kahneman the Nobel Prize in Economics. One aspect of this theory is that losses are twice as powerful, psychologically, as gains. That's hard to take, isn't it? This theory has very much played out in my life.

Fans of my first book (me, my mum, my bedroom door—as my book stops it from slamming) will know that I had a failed athletic career, which is surprising if you've ever seen me run. Sadly, losing has followed me as a fan of sports too. I swear I am the unluckiest spectator of all time. Now you might think I'm exaggerating, but I have stories to make you weep, with laughter or sadness, depend-ing on whether you are of high or low emotional intelligence.

Let me start with the basics. I've supported two teams in the last ten years that have had the most gut-wrenching bad luck or worst coaching you could ever believe. The first team is Derby County, a football team in England nicknamed the Rams, which has a glorious past that ended right around the time I started sup-porting them in the mid-1970s when I was six or seven years old. Since then, they have barely won anything. Worse, I have been to see them play live and they won two (yes, two!) of those twen-ty-four games (started crying yet?). Most of these games were on their home field too.

One of the worst defeats was when Derby County played at Wembley Stadium (the home of football) a few years ago in the play-off final. They lost in the last minute even though the other team was a man down and Derby had rained down on their goal for the last thirty minutes. Now this might not seem like a big deal, I guess, but please note I flew from Vancouver to London to watch this match; I spent roughly $3,000 to see one of the worst defeats you could imagine.

I said one of the worst, because I have an even better story for you. In 2016, England played in the European Football championships in France. The European Football championships are second only to the World Cup in ways in which English football fans can watch their team get humiliated.

Anyway, by chance, we managed to get front-row tickets to the round of sixteen (first knock-out game after the group stage). Now, even England always manages to get past this stage; generally, the better team gets the minnows in at this stage. So, it came to pass that England got Iceland—a team made up of shepherds, onion growers, and petty thieves who had to play for the national team in the dead of winter in Iceland as punishment (okay, this is not all quite true).

So here we are in gorgeous Nice on a warm and sunny evening, with front-row tickets to watch England play a team ranked 398th in the world. Well, you know what happens next, don't you? I won't share the resulting debacle, but there is a twist.

Before the game, my kids, Nesha, Callum, and Kian, painted their faces with the English flag.

At the end of the game, Callum started crying not just because England lost but because of the family he had been born into. As the tears streamed down, his facepaint ran and TV cameras from around the world captured him. It was the perfect shot. A young boy in the front row, face painted with the English flag, bawling his eyes out at another defeat. As soon as we got out the stadium, we had masses of texts from around the world telling us they just saw Callum sobbing live on TV. Callum was now the face of England's failure all around the world. The BBC, in particular, showed his face for months.

So, if you ever support a team that sucks, please don't shed a tear or tear your hair out. There is always someone worse off than you. And it's me.

5

Power of Expertise

"**O**KAY, EVERYONE, SQUEEZE in together!" shouted the photographer as all the passengers from the bus shuffled together, the Queenstown waterfront behind them.

"Winton, jump in at the front!" shouted Rory. "We can't have a group photograph without you!" Winton was reluctantly pushed into the photograph, given the Kiwi Experience sign, and the moment was captured forever.

The drivers of the buses are so powerful that passengers revere them by the end of the trip. I can even remember the name of my driver (Guess what? It was Winton!) twenty-six years after being on the bus.

A photo of KE passengers without the driver would not be a proper piece of memorabilia. Of course, a huge part of being a great driver is the relationships drivers build with the passengers, but this is not their main role. Their main role is to be an expert—an expert on New Zealand, an expert driver, and an expert host. KE leaders cultivate this expertise from day one.

All prospective drivers are taken on a "dummy" trip around New Zealand. They are asked to take notes of the various activities that are on offer and record any other information that may assist them in doing their job effectively. After this initial training, they are taken on a proper Kiwi Experience trip, where they observe how an experienced driver operates. The prospective drivers could be asked to take over the driving or the commentary at any moment. They are taken on as KE employees only if they perform satisfactorily in these two tests.

The driver uses their expertise to propel the experience to levels where passengers are willing to recommend them. Demonstrating expertise is crucial to every service encounter and it's the lifeblood of every service business.

Delivering expertise

Demonstrating expertise to the customer is the most important job of any service provider and how we execute the most important of the 3Rs—reliability. You can have all the frameworks you want, a fully accountable army of employees who have created the right context to deliver service, and your organization could still be lagging behind. It's tough to take, isn't it?

Customers don't just want your employees to be experts—they *need* your employees to be experts. And if your employees can't deliver that day in, day out with every customer and every interaction, then you will be a service slowcoach.

Fortunately, there is a huge body of science on

1. why expertise is the most important moment,
2. how to build our employees' expertise, and
3. how to create value *with* customers through our expertise.

As you will see, the science enables us to fully understand the depth of expertise's potency. Armed with this science, we are ready to deliver the most important moment of power.

Why is expertise so important?

There is always a moment during a customer's interaction with a business when they determine whether or not they are dealing with an expert. When an employee demonstrates that they *are* a reliable expert—they're knowledgeable, efficient, and professional, and they take ownership—is a moment that cannot be trumped. The same is true for internal service, when employees are serving each other.

As we know from chapter 2 on the 3Rs, the reliability and responsiveness of experts have long been shown to be the most important drivers of service quality, both internally and externally.[1] Employees who keep promises, are efficient, and perform the service correctly the first time have demonstrated the *most important* drivers of customers' perceptions of service excellence.

In chapter 2, I teased you with the 3Rs framework, but did you notice I did not give you a way to execute it? I merely stated it existed, as determined by scientific discoveries. Hands up if you were angry at me. Wow, so many of you! Okay, well, let's get on with it.

We execute reliability and responsiveness through the power of expertise. Experts are always reliable—they keep promises to shape trust. Experts are always building their knowledge (a key tenet of reliability), and they speak the customer's language (not talking down to them or in jargon), using their knowledge to help the customer achieve their goals—rather than achieving the employee's sales goals. Crucially, experts are always improving their ability to be accurate and to limit their mistakes.

Reliability is built around getting it right the first time, and experts are continuously looking for ways to build their credibility by being more precise.

Finally, experts are responsive—fast and efficient, they make it easy for customers to do business with you. They also take ownership of the customer experience and refuse, wherever possible, to ping-pong the customer around the organization. In summary, they are always working hard to reduce customers' effort and keep them informed along the journey.

Reliability and responsiveness, the most important of the 3Rs, are executed *consistently* by building your expertise and demonstrating it. Did I belabour this point? Good. I meant to.

But the power of expertise runs much deeper. One of the main reasons we follow experts is because it makes life easier when it comes to tough choices. As social scientists Kelton Rhoads and Robert Cialdini state, "When feeling overwhelmed by a complicated and consequential choice, most individuals still want a fully considered, point-by-point analysis of it—an analysis they may not be able to achieve except, ironically enough, through a shortcut: reliance on an expert. It is for this reason that a communicator's expertise becomes increasingly important as issues become increasingly complex."[2] So, as Rhoads and Cialdini suggest, following experts fulfills a cognitive function as well.

And it goes further still. As children, we are often raised to listen to people in positions of authority and follow their expertise—parents, teachers, and, in fact, anyone wearing a uniform (e.g., police officers and other members of the Village People). This deferral is so powerful that it has been given a name: Captainitis.[3] This term emerged when investigators from the Federal Aviation Administration noted that, on many occasions, an obvious mistake made by a captain was not rectified by other crew members. Despite clear evidence of the captain's error, crew members deferred to the expert and failed to correct or call attention to a captain's (often fatal) mistake.[4]

The Stanford Prison[5] experiments and the even more famous Stanley Milgram[6] research (which the BBC redid in 2009, with the exact same results) also highlight our willingness to follow authority. In both of these experiments, ordinary people, like us, inflict harm on others because they obey authority figures without thinking. These experiments show how much we defer a sense of responsibility to those in authority, even when they may not actually be an expert.

While these examples are negative (following experts in these cases has poor outcomes), the idea is that when we meet someone who we believe is an expert, we will generally follow them—and that is a good thing, as we must rely on experts to guide and help us for cognitive ease.

Building expertise

We cannot demonstrate expertise we don't have. This is where the power of expertise gets *really* exciting. I presume you don't share my excitement, but please bear with me. The science of expertise is truly life-changing, as it provides a whole new methodology that I believe could be used in schools, in businesses, and even at home.

Why is it so exciting? Well, first, virtually every organization is built on the opposite of these principles. Second, these principles are deeply rooted in more than thirty years of scientific discovery thanks mostly to a celebrated Swed, K. Anders Ericsson, professor of psychology at Florida State University, who is widely recognized as the world's leading theoretical and experimental researcher on expertise.

Ericsson presented his research in a book, *Peak* (written with Robert Pool). That book is far more important than this one and you should read it *immediately*. I feel like I'm on safe ground here, as you are up to chapter 5 and even if you read *Peak* before finishing this one, I know you will come back to me. Plus you've already paid for this book, so I really don't care if you finish it; I'm in Fiji right now living off the royalties. If you didn't buy this book and you are borrowing it from someone else, then please send five dollars as compensation—for my next cocktail—to Mark Colgate, Thatched Cabin 1, A Delicious Tropical Island, Paradise.

The whole notion of expertise revolves around what Ericsson calls "mental representations."[7] These representations are the ability of individuals to perform a task expertly without needing deliberate thought, because similar situations have been so well practiced that they *seem* second nature. In essence, they are preexisting patterns of information—facts, images, rules, relationships, and so on—that are held in long-term memory and can be used to respond quickly and effectively to certain types of situations.[8] These patterns have been created by having specific goals, practicing in a focused and determined manner, leaving one's comfort zone, and seeking and receiving feedback. We will explore these later in turn.

Ericsson argues that what sets experts apart is their quality and quantity of mental representations, which help them successfully navigate situations. Your role in becoming a service expert is to understand which representations to build (which will make you successful in your job and career) and then go through the process of building as many of these as you can. This could mean building representations that enable you to share your knowledge with the customer in the most effective way possible, to handle frustrated customers, to have great conversations with customers, to close a sale, or to do an effective needs analysis with a customer.

Even in call centres, this seems crucial. An examination of 150 insurance sales agents showed the agents who had undertaken "purposeful practice" showed they better understood "if/then" scenarios posed by customers than those who had not acquired these "knowledge structures."[9] This is because their insurance knowledge was better organized—the leading agents could figure out what to do more rapidly and precisely in any given situation, which made them more effective agents.[10]

My hypothesis here—and you should decide if you accept or reject this idea—is this: expertise is the foundation of exceptional service levels in organizations. Without expertise, customers are unlikely to be advocates for your brand. The main reason that expertise drives success in service is because it enables us to execute the reliability and responsiveness dimensions of quality in the eyes of customers.

We all must repeatedly go through this "expert" process if we are to avoid relying on our employees' "natural born" talents. In an interview with *The Psych Report*, Ericsson stated, "I'm not saying there wouldn't be genetic factors [that drive expertise], but what I would say is that we currently don't have robust evidence that there are these genetic factors."[11] This quote should be on every employee's and leader's desk, cubicle, and bicycle. There is no science that shows there are "service genes" that make some people better equipped than others to deliver great service. There *is* a science to delivering great service, and if you use this science, you will set yourself apart from those who don't.

Four steps to expertise

A key part of this science is Ericsson's methodology of growing expertise through purposeful practice.

1. **Purposeful practice has very defined, specific goals.** If you are working on ambiguous goals (for example, to improve your ability

to serve customers), or if you have too many goals, then you are unlikely to achieve much of anything. A limited number of specific, time-bound, and measurable goals means there is a higher probability of achieving those goals than if they are vague or there's a long laundry list.

2. **Purposeful practice is focused and determined.** Employees must give practice their full attention and persist over time and in the face of setbacks. If you're not *consciously* practicing the things you need to improve on and persisting with this effort, then you will not achieve these goals. Becoming an expert is a journey that requires resilience and grit. By ensuring that employees understand the effort required and encouraging them to persist, you will be more likely to set yourself apart from the competition.

3. **Purposeful practice requires leaving one's comfort zone.** If employees aren't pushing themselves beyond what is comfortable and familiar, they will not advance. Our tendency is to focus on and practice the things that we already excel at because it makes us feel good. Ericsson's research is clear—we will not improve unless we are always operating at the edge of our current skills and pushing those limits.

4. **Purposeful practice involves feedback.** Immediate, specific feedback on where employees are falling short is vital. Ericsson's research consistently talks about the importance of having a coach—someone who encourages you to set specific goals, believes in you, and gives you feedback on the progress you are making and the areas that you can improve. Without a coach, becoming an expert is extremely difficult. Think about athletes trying to reach world-class levels—not many of them would believe they could make it without a coach. We shouldn't believe it either.

As Ericsson and Pool say, "The right kind of practice carried out over a sufficient period of time will lead to improvement. Nothing else will."[12]

This process is integral to growing our customer service expertise. It's also the process the people that we lead must follow. As stated before, our education system and organizations don't follow these steps, which results in incredibly inefficient training methods. Think about the times at school, university, and work when you were exposed to the above structure. I'm guessing it was almost never.

One reason for this is that we live in a feedback-free world: we rarely receive feedback on how we are doing, or how we could grow. Feedback we do get is often too late to make a difference. Think of feedback you received *after* you handed in an assignment at university (how useless is post-hoc feedback which accompanies a grade?) or performance reviews ("Couldn't you have told me that nine months ago?").

Ultimately, most training (service training included) revolves around memorization, which doesn't build mental representations but stores learning in our short-term memory. Think of spelling tests—ultimately a useless exercise. You might learn the word in time for a test, but because the word is out of context (it is not written in a story, for example) or broken down in a way so it can be recalled easily, you'll forget the correct spelling shortly after.

Also think of how quickly we learn a language when we have to survive in a new country. I learned French in school for six years (probably more than 400 hours of tutoring) and I can recall almost nothing. If they had dropped me in Bordeaux as an eleven-year-old on my own, I would have been fluent in six weeks. I would also have become a damn good connoisseur of wine.

There is a far better way. Think of how productive and efficient our education systems and organizations would be if people continually went through the cycle of purposeful practice. Let's pick any skill—like running a great meeting inside an organization. Virtually everyone has to run meetings at some point in their lives, and many people go on training courses to learn how to run them effectively. But the most productive way of improving would be for a coach to observe you running a meeting, and you'd then collaborate and work with that person on areas to improve. Then you practice things that you find difficult, which will make a difference over time. You would get the coach to observe you again and give you additional feedback. The things that you practice should take you outside of your comfort zone (for example, using new techniques to encourage quiet people in the meeting to contribute and limit the contribution of dominating attendees). This cycle may go on for a few months.

Some professions do this really well in training. Students who go to journalism school get endless feedback on the articles they write, which mimics the four steps of purposeful practice perfectly, but those who go through this *after* they have qualified get very little feedback. Think doctors, educators, tradespeople, leaders of any kind, realtors, car mechanics, customer-service professionals, and so on.

By adopting this approach, you and your employees will grow in ways other organizations are not, giving you an edge. Also, this is the only process that you should go through if you want your employees to increase their service levels. Otherwise, you may find that they will plateau and their performance will stay the same.

Wow, I am so passionate about this I could write a book on it... Hold on, I did! *8 Moments of Power in Coaching* is waiting for you if you want to take this further.

Creating value with customers

Our job is to use our expertise so that we are creating value *with* customers. There is a crucial difference between creating value *with* customers and believing you create value *for* customers. Customers must be considered co-creators of value.[13]

We cannot create value for customers; we can only create value with them when they use our service in a way that fulfills their needs easily. One of the best quotes on this notion I have read is from Cordell Ratzlaff, a former executive at Apple and now the user experience director at Google: "People don't use the computer to enjoy the operating system... They use a computer because they want to create something... The computer is just a tool... It's about what people want to do... You have to know who these people are and what they're really trying to accomplish."[14] When you know your customer and create something that helps them accomplish their goals, then you are creating value *with* them.

There is no value created until a customer co-creates the service with you. Before then, only potential value exists. By asking questions to understand customer needs, listening carefully, sharing our knowledge in ways in which they comprehend, and then customizing the experience to fulfill their needs, we will then be creating value *with* them. In a service context, knowledge and skills are the underlying sources of value. This is why we need to grow our expertise so much.

Think of a realtor you have hired to help you buy a house. Picture the realtor carefully listening to your needs, showing you only those houses that are appropriate for you, making the buying experience seem effortless, and finally finding a house that is just right for you. In this context, they are creating value with you, unlike a realtor who sends you endless listings, takes you to houses that you would never buy, and makes the buying process extremely painful. There is little value created in that context.

This new way of thinking is important as customers are increasingly able to access an immense amount of information. They can inform themselves and then share their experiences, skills, and opinions with others. Hence, they tend to be more knowledgeable, demanding, and networked.[15] Customers are ultimately able to make more informed decisions, assess value on their own terms, influence the expectations of other customers, and generally decide for themselves how they want to interact with a firm. Communication once flowed almost entirely from firms to customers, but customer feedback is continuously increasing. In this environment, the role of the customer has changed from "isolated" to "connected," from "unaware" to "informed," and from "passive" to "active."[16]

So, our job is to use our skills and knowledge (i.e., our expertise) to create value with customers in ways they can't do for themselves.

Creating value through your expertise

After an exhaustive search of the literature and my own experience as a researcher and practitioner, I have determined there are four parts to creating value through expertise:

1. fulfilling customers' needs—delivering on your core promise,
2. consuming as much TOFU as possible,
3. using your knowledge and skills—asking questions, listening hard, and
4. giving customers cognitive control.

Fulfilling customers' needs

Trust and credibility with brands and individuals are built if you are fulfilling customers' needs and keeping your promises. As we will see in the Amazon case study below, you can separate yourself from the competition by identifying what your core customers' needs are and satisfying them better than anyone else. Amazon identified three main customer needs and met them in an exceptional way. They managed to do this very early on in their history—it just took them a long time to make money from it. When investigating the Amazon case, you'll truly come to understand how persistent they were in executing on these core needs and how much they believed in their mission (correction: how much Jeff Bezos got employees to believe).

The challenge is to work out what exactly it means for your organization to fulfill your customers' needs. Meeting needs for guests of a budget hotel looks very different from meeting needs for guests of a luxury hotel. YouTube's success was that it was the first to figure out that the instant upload of videos was the core need it had to fulfill. It made a previously difficult thing much, much easier by combining technological advances. Before YouTube, sharing a video on the web was basically, "Hey, check out this video! *buffering... buffering...*," and it was very painful.

What we know is that reliability is built around consistent performance—fulfilling core promises, being accurate, and solving customers' problems to build confidence and credibility. Becoming the most trusted brand in your industry requires you to do this better than anyone else.

TOFU

One of the key disciplines at the Commonwealth Bank—which changed everything in terms of excellence in delivering service—was the core behaviour of TOFU.

Not to be confused with rubbery food, the TOFU I am referring to stands for **t**aking **o**wnership and **f**ollowing **u**p. (The FU in most other organizations is something quite different.) This mantra was for use not just with the customer but with each other as well; we recognized that delivering service excellence to our peers was a prerequisite to delivering service excellence to the customer. By taking ownership of the customer experience, you are much more likely to create value for the customer.

TOFU has three ways it can be activated. First, imagine a customer has an inquiry that you cannot answer. In this context, you do whatever you can to not ping-pong the customer around the organization. Instead, you take ownership to find out the answer yourself and then follow up with the customer, so they do not have to do the work themselves. Remember how it feels to hear the line, "Oh, I'm sorry I can't help you. I will have to pass you off to Jonathan in finance." Now Jonathan may be very nice, but the first-person resolution is always better.

The second way to activate TOFU is when you have to pass the customer off to another employee because it is not your domain of expertise. If you did try to fulfill the customer's request, it would just create more confusion. In this context, you would do a warm handover to an employee and explain to the employee what that customer was looking for (rather than making the customer re-explain it) to ensure a smooth transition. If the second employee is away from their desk or with another customer, you would leave a message or send an email to them about the need to contact this customer. Then you would follow up with the employee in a reasonable timeframe to make sure they had done the follow-up with the customer; otherwise, the ball would likely be dropped and the customer left with a bad experience.

The third way to activate TOFU is when a customer has a problem or a complaint. TOFU is never more important than when a customer complains. I will discuss this in detail in chapter 7, but at the Commonwealth Bank of Australia, we knew that TOFU was critical here because when a customer's problem is successfully handled, their perception of the bank immediately changes.

Activating TOFU in these three scenarios drove the Commonwealth Bank to number one in customer satisfaction. This behaviour was reinforced by the organization through continual programs, communication, and feedback. A few times throughout the year, there would be service and sales meetings explicitly focused on TOFU (see chapter 9 about the role of these meetings) to ensure that everyone in the organization knew the importance of this discipline and how to execute it on a daily basis.

In terms of feedback, we did quarterly internal customer surveys to track how well we were doing. To monitor the quality of the service we delivered to external customers, we also did an additional 3,000 surveys per week with customers who came into the branch or called the call centre. Every single one of those surveys had a question on it to measure TOFU (for example, "Did the employee take ownership of your experience?"), so we could monitor the progress of that behaviour and provide feedback to each team.

Knowledge and skills

Another foundational part of expertise, and the one we can coach the most, is knowledge. This relates to your expertise as a leader, salesperson, service representative, educator, negotiator, or any of the thousands of other jobs where technical skills and knowledge enable you to fulfill customers' needs and answer their questions competently. Another big part here is knowing where your knowledge stops, so that you can pass the customer off to someone with even more expertise.

Encouraging employees to fake their expertise is not a great long-term approach.

Crucially, we must also coach toward understanding "the curse of knowledge."[17] The theory of the curse of knowledge shows why an individual who knows something deeply finds it hard to view a situation through the eyes of someone without this knowledge. It is difficult for them to relate to others who do not share their knowledge, as they do not remember a time when they didn't know it themselves. This is important because as someone grows their expertise, they often end up talking down to the customer, using acronyms or language customers simply do not understand. You can probably remember an experience visiting a doctor who didn't explain things in lay terms—because of the curse of knowledge.

Experts are always growing their expertise, learning better ways to share their knowledge, and avoiding the curse of knowledge—this enables them to create value with their customers.

Cognitive control

The final part of creating value with customers is to give customers control. Customers love feeling in control, even when they can't control the outcome. Whenever you take this approach, you are giving customers the gift of cognitive control.[18]

There are two kinds of control: behavioural and cognitive. Behavioural control is when you can give customers control over their choices or outcomes. For example, a financial planner gives you a choice of risk profiles for your investments. Giving customers behavioural control is always the preferred option as this gives customers the strongest feeling of control.

However, in many cases, we can't give customers behavioural control (because we are the experts and so must make many decisions on the customer's behalf and control many processes), but we can give them information, which gives them cognitive control. Cognitive control creates value with customers: they are at cognitive ease when they understand their role in the service delivery, know how long the process will be, are informed of any delays in the process (before they find out themselves), and receive clear explanations as to what's happening. Think about working through a medical issue with a specialist, say, for a sense of how valuable cognitive control can be.

Also, think of when you track a courier package as it travels across the world. You have no actual control as to whether the package will arrive safely and on time. However, you feel so much more confident and comfortable if you can go online and find out where your package is at that moment and its estimated arrival time. This is what experts do, and what you must do if you want to be perceived as an expert in your domain.

When a customer (whether an internal or external customer) walks away from an interaction with an employee believing that employee has taken ownership of the interaction, possessed the requisite knowledge, fulfilled their core needs, and even managed to pass on some of their insight to the customer—then, as the employee, you have achieved what every great service provider does: you have created value with the customer.

Amazon does this better than any other company I know.

CASE STUDY: Amazon

EVERY SELF-RESPECTING SERVICE book needs an Amazon case study. Amazon is well known for its ability to fulfill customers' needs, becoming the most trusted brand in the world. I think this is one of the most remarkable things about Amazon—even though it is an online company with very little direct interaction with a customer, it still manages to create trust. It has received countless awards.[19]

Amazon's success is based on the most basic principle of all: understand customers' fundamental needs and fulfill them in a way that makes it *very easy* for customers to do business with you. If you have ever used Amazon, you know exactly what I mean. While this seems like common sense, Amazon excels at knowing what these needs are and creates a culture around always delivering them and continually improving at implementing them.

Reliability: Fulfilling customer needs

"We know that customers want low prices. We know customers want fast delivery. We also know that customers want a big selection. And those things are going to be true ten years from now; these things are going to be true twenty years from now. So, we count on those things and we can put energy into them."[20] Jeff Bezos has repeated this message incessantly.

Employees at Amazon know that succeeding in these three areas is what they must consistently do. Amazon will sell a product to the customer at a loss to ensure it is competitive. As Bezos says, "Why should a customer pay for our inefficiency?" Now, of course, in the long run, if Amazon can't make money from a product, it will stop selling it. But it knows that fulfilling the customer's needs comes before short-term profitability. This way of thinking is very far from many organizations, which won't lose money on one transaction, let alone many.

In terms of always succeeding on fast delivery, Bezos states, "We're not satisfied until it's 100 percent."[21] In December 2011, Bezos was "very proud" that Amazon was able to hit the inconceivable goal of delivering on his promise to get packages to 99.9 percent of customers before Christmas—no small feat transporting millions of packages worldwide and missing their mark on a handful of deliveries in just a few, short nights.

Bezos is even stricter about what customers don't want. They hate delays, defects, and out-of-stock products. The metrics team at Amazon constantly tracks reliability. It speaks volumes that Amazon tracks its performance against about 500 measurable goals but nearly 80 percent relate to customer objectives. Some Amazonians try to reduce out-of-stock merchandise; others race to build a bigger library of downloadable movies.[22]

This obsession with reliability and metrics creates alignment and momentum within Amazon. Fulfilling customers' needs becomes habitual when you have this extreme focus. There is no better example of this extreme focus than Bezos leaving an empty chair at the conference table and letting attendees know it's occupied by "the most important person in the room": the customer.

Using knowledge to make better customer decisions

As we know, the heart of expertise is knowledge. Using knowledge to create value with customers is what Amazon does well. All of Amazon's departments are completely data-driven, based upon the success and failures of the customer experience. This allows Amazon to take risks to innovate and make difficult decisions based on concrete evidence as to what is best for the customer and, ultimately, what is best for the company.

In an interview with *Forbes*, Bezos said this of his customer-centric company: "We don't focus on the optics of the next quarter; we focus on what is going to be good for customers. I think this aspect of our culture is rare."[23] He continues, "Customer obsession is not just listening to customers; customer obsession is also inventing on their behalf. Because it's not their job to invent for themselves and so you need to be an inventor and pioneer."[24]

Amazon is continually using its knowledge of its customers to make better decisions on their behalf, inventing on their behalf (Amazon Prime is a great example), and designing processes that are more efficient and more reliable, which, in turn, expedites profitability for Amazon.

Cognitive control

As a matter of course, Amazon sends confirmation emails after receiving orders and almost immediately thereafter sends another email with tracking information. You can keep up with incoming purchases every step of the journey.

You can also look up your purchase history, going back to your very first purchase. I just looked up three books I bought back in 2004, including the classic *Alexander and the Terrible, Horrible, No Good, Very Bad Day*. You can write a review of the items you purchased, leave feedback about the packaging, and (if still in the timeframe) return and/or replace items easily.

Amazon puts you in control even before you purchase. Its products are extensively reviewed, creating confidence in the buyer. If you are buying from a third-party seller (of which there are thousands), you can check their reviews to ensure you are buying from a reputable vendor.

The opportunities to understand the quality of the product, know the reliability of the seller before they commit, be entirely informed about the delivery process, and rate, return, and review everything—even packaging!—gives customers a strong perception of control.

Taking ownership

Jeff Bezos still receives many customer complaints personally. A famous example of taking ownership was in 2009 when Amazon remotely deleted copies of the books *1984* and *Animal Farm* from users' Kindles. The incident prompted an online outcry from customers who saw the dark "Big Brother" side of Amazon—one that Bezos had worked hard to steer clear of. Amazon quickly made an apology, but it was a relatively dry and robotic statement from the press team, which Jeff Bezos was not happy with. He quickly sent an informal and heartfelt apology to replace it. See below.[25]

Jeffery P. Bezos says:

This is an apology for the way we previously handled illegally sold copies of 1984 and other novels on Kindle. Our "solution" to the problem was stupid, thoughtless, and painfully out of line with our principles. It is wholly self-inflicted, and we deserve the criticism we've received. We will use the scar tissue from this painful mistake to help make better decisions going forward, ones that match our mission.

With deep apology to our customers,

Jeff Bezos
Founder & CEO
Amazon.com

Customers reacted like this:

> **Bryan L. Wheeler** says:
>
> That took a lot of courage Mr. Bezos. Still a very loyal Amazon customer here. :)
>
> **Luv2Reads** says:
>
> Wow! Thanks so much. This speaks volumes about Amazon. My loyalty keeps getting stronger. :)
>
> **Paul Dyer** says:
>
> I have canceled my kindle subscriptions as a result of your "solution". This is the most honest and thoughtful apology I have ever heard from a large corp., as a result, I will reactivate my subscription immediately. Thanks, Jeff, for your post.

Does it get any better than this in terms of TOFU?

Amazon knows that problems can be devastating in the age of viral tweets and blogs. Bezos asks thousands of Amazon managers, including himself, to attend two days of call-centre training *each year*. The payoff: humility and empathy for the customer.[26]

Through careful choices and clever use of information, you can demonstrate expertise with every customer *and*, with the right culture, grow this expertise constantly.

Recap

Now you know the most important moment of power. Please sit back in your chair and breathe a deep sigh of relief. Yes, it feels good, doesn't it?

Okay, that's enough. There is work to do.

I said STOP!

Please recall the key elements of expertise—using purposeful practice to grow your expertise, using TOFU to demonstrate this expertise, and being proactive in using cognitive control to pass some of your expertise to the customer.

Even though we have done the most important moment of power, we still have two to go, so don't get complacent. Next, you and I need to build relationships; yes, a deep relationship. Shall we start with a walk together and see how it goes from there? Oops, wrong context. I mean, let's start by examining how to build strong connections with customers in the next chapter.

And then maybe we can go for that walk?

6

Power of Relationships

"THAT MĀORI HĀNGI group meal was so much fun," Rory said to Winton. "Having locals help us make a traditional meal was a great way to meet other people on the bus too."

"Rotorua is a very special place, with a special smell," Winton said and laughed. "We love getting passengers together. We've had many passengers marry after meeting on Kiwi Experience—we are that good at it!"

"Well, I didn't meet anyone that special last night, but there are certainly lots of like-minded people," said Rory. "It is just hard to meet them on normal bus trips."

"I promise you I will find you a life partner by the end of the trip," said Winton, winking. "And even that is included in the price."

Market research has shown that the interaction between the customers on the bus is the second most important part of a Kiwi Experience trip (after the driver). Backpackers generally get a kick out of meeting other travellers like them. In fact, many backpackers travel for the specific purpose of making new friends and acquaintances. It is important for KE to ensure this happens by managing customer interactions well. Emotional connection does not necessarily have to come from the employee and the customer—by creating connections between customers, we can also build a relationship between the customer and the brand.

Kiwi Experience does several things to achieve the correct customer mix on its buses and ensure that the customers interact well together (beyond the normal interaction that would occur). First, it ensures, as best as it can, that its booking agents do not book people who would be ill suited to the kind of experiences offered. For example, older travellers may not be interested in some of the things that Kiwi Experience does. This strategy prevents potential customers from having a negative experience. Such an experience could influence the enjoyment of other customers on the same bus and ultimately lead to negative word-of-mouth. The company sends representatives from its booking agents on tour to help them understand the types of people who would enjoy travelling with KE; this also ensures they are educated representatives.

Second, at an early stage of the trip, the driver encourages social interaction among the riders and enables them to form bonds and friendships. This has a positive impact on the quality of customers' experiences and their overall impression. The drivers encourage interaction through group meals, social activities in the evening (e.g., fancy dress competitions), and booking all backpacker accommodation for passengers, which generally means customers stay with each other in the best hostels en route.

There is no doubt this creative approach creates strong friendships on the bus and, in many cases, creates friendships for life. There are many stories of passengers who marry after meeting on the KE bus, with the wedding party including other KE passengers too.

Building strong relationships between customers, as well as between employees and customers, creates a strong emotional connection to the brand—one that often separates that brand from the competition.

Moment of quandary

I've been trying to think of a snappy title for this moment of power for years. So far, we have power of context and power of expertise, which are thought-provoking names that summarize really well what needs to happen in these "moments." My hesitation with the "relationships" title is two-fold. First, it's such an overused term that it's lost some of its meaning. Second, do we want to *build* a relationship with every customer? Is a warm service encounter really all we need?

Ultimately, I think we need to be true to the science of service presented in chapter 2. The relationship dimension revolves around treating customers as unique and special, giving caring and personalized attention, and showing customers they are understood and valued.[1] While we may not want to develop profound relationships with all customers, as it's not possible or cost effective, we certainly want strong relationships with all customers.

Every organization—whether big or small, online or offline, continuously interacting with the customer or rarely interacting with the customer—needs to deliver service that cares for the customer, personalizes the experience, makes them feel important, and shows that they are understood and valued. The process of building strong relationships allows these things to happen in every context.

The research I presented in chapter 2 (figure 2.3) shows that relationship building is the great differentiator in getting customers to rate your service nine out of ten. Being reliable and responsive will get you a long way, but executing on the relationship dimension enables you to drive positive word-of-mouth to exceptional levels.

Many companies are reliable, are responsive, and do the basics very well. There are very few organizations, however, that execute on the relationship dimension *as well as* the reliability and responsiveness dimensions, which is why building strong relationships enables you to create a strong brand that is unique in relation to others. Again, it's important to remember that building strong relationships without being reliable and responsive is unlikely to make a huge impact.

Relationship building only gets the shine it deserves when you are reliable and responsive as well.

Three ways to build relationships

1. Like the one you are with,
2. Personalize the experience, and
3. Go first.

1. Like the one you are with

How long does it take you to decide if an employee wants to serve you in a face-to-face context, on the phone, live chat, or email? We are primed to immediately recognize the tone of their message, the warmth (or lack thereof) in their voice, and their body language.

No amount of training will overcome a lack of interest in the customer. It's all about the employee's mindset—*they must always like the one they are with*. Whether remotely or face-to-face, your job is to always build and maintain this mindset in yourself and your team, if you lead one. Again, the same is true for your co-workers—always remind yourself that your colleagues are your customers too, and that you need to build the culture of service by delivering high-quality service to them. The whirlwind of the workplace means you can easily forget about the customer and focus on your needs. By building in interventions, you can always draw your attention back to the customer.

When I first arrived at the Commonwealth Bank, one of my jobs was to define bright spots in the organization—employees or teams that were already delivering world-class service that we could learn from and replicate. One employee got my attention because she received more customer compliments than anyone else in the bank, which was an incredible achievement given there were 20,000 people working on the front line. She worked in the call centre in Newcastle, about two hours north of Sydney. I jumped in the car and drove to meet her. When I finally had a chance to sit down and talk to her, she literally had a stack of customer compliments on her desk (this was 2007 when people still wrote actual letters).

I asked her how she did it, and she said, "It's my mindset. When I hear the click of a new customer coming through [she took about 120–150 calls a day], I imagine it's a long-lost friend. The tone of my voice is warm and I'm curious; this is a fantastic way to start every call."

This is a great example of the power of mindset. You "like the one that you are with" when you have a positive mindset with each and every customer; from there, it is so much easier to build relationships. If you don't have this mindset from the beginning, then building a strong relationship is so much harder.

Born into poverty, Joe Girard sold 13,001 cars over the course of his fifteen-year career. He holds the Guinness World Record for being the world's greatest salesman. How did Joe Girard get this title? The main answer is his mindset.

Joe Girard did an excellent interview with the *Harvard Business Review* a few years ago.[2] At one point, the interviewer asks, "You say you love your customers. What if they aren't so likable?" Joe replies, "It's like a marriage. You need to like each other. And if you treat people right, you will love them." His point is, just like a marriage, you get out of the customer relationship what you put in.

Joe Girard goes on to tell a powerful story about how he was poor and needed his customers to make a purchase just so he could survive. "What I saw was a bag of groceries walking toward me. I literally got down on my hands and knees and begged, and I made my first sale. The customer said that with everything he had bought over the years—insurance, houses, cars—he had never seen anyone beg like that. Then I borrowed ten dollars from my boss against my commission and bought food for my family. I appreciate every person who bought from me so much."[3] This point is key. Even when he became wealthy, he kept this mindset going. He could have become complacent, as many successful people and firms do, but he did not.

Finally, Joe talks about how important it is to treat colleagues like customers. When customers came back with a problem with their car, he got mechanics to fix the issue immediately. "I made a deal with a nice Italian restaurant, and every third Wednesday I would take all of the service people to dinner—the people who wrote up the service orders, mechanics, the parts department, everyone. I would eat with them and tell them how much I appreciated them."[4] The insight here is that it's rare to deliver service on your own; you have to nourish and refresh the spirit of the people around you by treating them as if they were the customer.

We must always renew our mindsets to build strong relationships. Think about orientation programs at organizations—virtually all of them talk about the importance of the customer and how to serve and build relationships with them, but active methods to keep this growth mindset about the customer stop there. There are no persistent methods for highlighting the importance of the customer, inspiring employees to raise their service game, and building commitments with employees to always deliver great service. Without these, it is doubtful employees will always "like the one they are with."

Chapter 8 further describes how to build and endure the customer growth mindset in the long run—quite romantically too.

2. Personalize the experience

The secret ingredient to building strong relationships is to make the customer feel important. This is easy once you personalize the experience. Personalization must make the customer feel special; otherwise, you have wasted your time. How many times have you seen the robotic use of personalization? Printed messages in holiday cards, rather than handwritten, or the customer's name used endlessly in a call centre context because the employee has been told to say the customer's name at least seventy-seven times. We reject these attempts at personalization because they are not about us. So, when you are personalizing the experience with the customer, it is about making an impact with them and building the relationship, because you genuinely want to make them feel special.

You are only limited by your imagination in terms of how you can personalize the experience of individual customers. Well-documented and researched techniques for building personal relationships with customers are: remembering birthdays or other special events,[5] using the customer's name in a genuinely meaningful way,[6] spending a day in the life of your customers,[7] knowing the customer's history with the firm (using CRM data usually) to recall key events and purchases or to create consistency across channels,[8] and finally having a pleasant conversation with the customer.[9]

I would like, however, to focus on the methods that stand out as being more potent and novel than the rest. These are personalization through similarities and connections, a "backstage pass," compliments, and uncommonly attentive behaviour.

Similarities and connections

People, in general, engage with others who are like them. So, whether you live in the same town or you both have kids, similarities allow our customers to think of you as a person, not just another employee. Here are two ways to do this:

1. **Identify common interests:** You both like travelling, have the same hobby, follow the same sports team, just purchased a new home, have the same parents—the list of opportunities to discover common interests is endless. The better the questions you ask, the easier it will be to find that common connection. The science of social psychology is clear: customers like employees who are *like* them.[10]

2. **Be yourself:** By allowing your charisma and personality to shine, you can also make your clients feel more connected to the organization and to you as a person, making your service a pleasant experience. The science shows that employees that make the customers smile because of a charismatic, humorous, or friendly interaction build much rapport.[11]

A "backstage pass"

Another ingenious way to customize the experience is to give customers exclusivity. Nothing feels better than when you have access to activities, information, and experiences others do not.

Queensland Tourism in Australia recently produced an excellent article on how to create memorable experiences, highlighting the power of the backstage pass.[12] Obviously, this requires some creativity, but the effect can be profound.

Here are a few ways to do this:

- exclusive deals and specials to certain customers,
- sharing tips that only locals know (e.g., a great hike),
- information that puts customers in control of their experience (i.e., advice that helps them make better choices),
- access to products, service, and experiences others don't have access to, or
- squeezing a customer in for a late appointment.

"Backstage passes" are great ways to reward loyal and important customers; by their very nature, the perks should not be for everyone. A good example is American Express's extremely successful Front of the Line access for certain cardholders so they get tickets for events before anyone else.

Compliments

Research shows that praise and other forms of positive recognition also build relationships.[13] Knowing that someone appreciates us can be a highly effective way to build a connection.

Hands up if you love it when a customer praises or recognizes you, as an employee, for doing something really well. All of you. I thought so. Well, I am here to tell you the science of relationship building shows that customers also love it when they get a sincere and genuine compliment from an employee for something they have done. You need to always be on the front foot in looking for ways to praise the customer.

When I got to the Commonwealth Bank, I recommended that we look for more opportunities to sincerely compliment our customers.

Thankfully, my superior told me that this was too risky without researching it beforehand. So, in three branches in Sydney (one out west, one on the north shore, and one in the heart of the city), we ended our conversations with customers in one of three ways. The teller randomly selected the A, B, or C ending. A was no compliment, B was a loyalty compliment ("Thanks for your loyalty to the bank"), and C was a personal compliment, which the tellers chose: "Thanks for being so lovely to serve; it's been a pleasure." Now bizarrely, all of the tellers, in all of the three branches, were women. I don't know why and I can't explain it, but it did make doing research a lot easier, as all of the tellers felt comfortable using this personal compliment with both female and male customers. (Male tellers may have had difficulty using this compliment with male customers.)

The table below highlights the results with 500 customers, a very tasty sample. We hired an external market research team to stop customers on the way out of the branch after they had one of the three endings. This research took us many weeks as obviously not all customers got compliments (so we could not research them) and many customers who were part of the research (but did not know it) refused the survey on the way out.

As has been the theme for this book, we only measured excellence—that is the percentage of customers who gave us a nine or ten in the satisfaction survey. This was consistent with how we were measuring satisfaction across the bank.

Table 6.1: The power of compliments

EXPERIMENTAL GROUP	RESULT—OVERALL 9S AND 10S
No compliment	38% (N=165)
Loyalty compliment ("Thanks for your loyalty to the bank")	43% (N=166)
Personal compliment ("Thanks for being so lovely to serve, it has been a pleasure")	66% (N=169) The differences are statistically significant from groups above.

As you can see from table 6.1, there was no meaningful difference between the first two groups. This makes sense because a loyalty compliment basically means "thanks for giving us cash." Now if you reward someone for their loyalty, like giving them a quarter of a percentage points off the mortgage rate because of their long-term relationship with the bank, that's a different story.

However, the group that got the personal compliment had a much higher percentage of nines and tens, which was statistically significant. This highlights the impact of genuine and sincere compliments. Moving from 38 percent to 66 percent is huge—28 percentage points huge, actually. Our results were consistent with the research on the potency of compliments.[14]

Please remember this and encourage your employees (and yourself) to give customers compliments that are warm and sincere.

However, for every yin, there is a yang. Unfortunately, what happened in a few cases was that when a female teller gave a male customer a compliment, he thought she was flirting with him and in turn wrote his phone number on a deposit slip and passed it to her. We were astonished as the teller was only giving the male customer a pleasant compliment. We now appreciated two things from this research. One, compliments are powerful. Two, men are sleazebags. But then perhaps you knew that already.

Uncommonly attentive behaviour

The final way to personalize the experience is through atypical attention toward the customer. Two exceptional service researchers, Dwayne Gremler and Kevin Gwinner, undertook research on 824 relationship-building interactions between customers and employees and identified that attentiveness "appears instrumental in the development of rapport between the employee and the customer."[15] Not only did these researchers identify, in prior studies, that "simply being attentive to others can build rapport," but in their research "uncommonly attentive behavior" *was the largest category by far*. Twenty-nine percent of all interactions that were considered by customers to build relationships were categorized as "uncommonly attentive behavior." Clearly, showing attention is a significant part of relationship building.

In terms of specifics, the dominant theme in this category was "atypical action behavior," which the researchers say includes "situations in which the customer perceives that the employee has gone out of his or her way or above and beyond the call of duty"[16] to respond to the customer's situation or to please the customer. Respondents believe these actions help the employee establish a relationship with them. A good example from this research was a customer—in recounting a visit to a clothing retailer—who said, "I told [the employee] what type of clothing items I was looking for, and she gave me some suggestions and took me around the store. She helped me find sizes and went out of her way to call other stores to find some items they no longer had in stock."[17]

Other researchers refer to such atypical employee actions as "extra-role customer service," which they describe as "discretionary behaviours of contact employees in serving customers that extend beyond formal role requirements." They contend that such behaviours, including those in which employees go out of their way or beyond the call of duty for customers, often lead to customer delight and relationship building.[18]

Again, there are simply hundreds of ways to show atypical attention, such as listening carefully, walking customers to the door, coming out from the behind the desk to greet them, following up calls to make sure everything went as expected, answering questions, offering suggestions to customers, or creating surprise gestures toward the customer (like the Ironman cake story I shared earlier).

Highlighting the importance of showing customers attention must be a key part of employee training and coaching.

CASE STUDY: Lloyd Daser and Pan Pacific Hotels

LLOYD DASER RUNS two Pan Pacific Hotels (sister hotels just 500 metres apart) in Whistler, British Columbia. One of these hotels, the Village Centre, was rated the number one resort by *Condé Nast Traveler* in 2017. The team at the Pan Pacific Whistler consistently delivers reliable and responsive service and receives customer satisfaction survey results and social media rankings in the ninety-plus percentile. They achieve this through ongoing training, coaching, and embracing their own brand standards. However, where they excel is in building relationships.

I've stayed in both hotels, and the rooms and the service genuinely make you feel like you are in a home away from home. Given my experience, I wanted to know how they always manage to stick the landing and make it such a special experience. What "interventions" do they use to ensure the stay is personalized? How do they use coaching and observations? How do they use technology to foster relationships? The answer to these questions might surprise you.

Daser and his team use coaching, technology, and interventions to build relationships, but that's only a tiny part of the story. Virtually all of their relationship building happens because they have built the right environment. As Daser states, "We create a culture of family for employees and customers. In terms of the guest experience/relationship building, the focus is on each customer as if they were a guest in our home (as opposed to a hotel). It is a different type of experience and mindset, and great for building lasting relationships." Now, this sounds like something every GM of a hotel might say, but read on to learn how Daser actually builds this culture.

"When I opened the Pan Pacific Kuala Lumpur International Airport hotel, most of the people we hired were from the small villages around the airport outside of Kuala Lumpur. They had never flown on or even been on an airplane. It was impossible for them to even begin to understand how our arriving guests would feel after getting off a long-haul flight. So we did a deal with Malaysia Airlines to use their training facility and a full-sized airplane cabin, which they had on site to train their cabin crew, as part of our training. We put all of our team through a simulated flight where they had to sit on the airplane for sixteen hours like a real passenger. They got to watch movies, take advantage of other in-flight services, and use the toilets... just like a real passenger. There was a lot of fun and excitement at first, but by hour sixteen they were more than ready to get off and had a fabulous appreciation (without ever leaving the ground) of how our guests felt when they arrived at the hotel. We ended the day with everyone getting to exit down the emergency slide!"

Is this not the best story you have ever heard? This is how you build relationships—by genuinely putting yourself in your customers' shoes (or, in this case, airplane slippers). As mentioned in chapter 5, great service providers don't think *about* their customers, they think *like* them. This is a great example of how to think *like* them.

Essentially, Daser leads through cultural norms. This is where inter-personal relationships and teamwork regulate employee behaviour. Employees develop the means for their own decision-making and initiatives through these cultural norms. This method of leadership can work extremely well in service contexts.

Leading through values

To build relationships, leaders must lead from the front. If you are not willing to work extremely hard to build relationships with employees and customers as a servant leader, then the culture will never support the extra mile required to do this better than any other competing hotel.

The idea is that successful service businesses are built on the alignment between target customers' needs and the design of the firm's operating system. In businesses which depend on human interaction for success—which is most service businesses—the types of beliefs and values instilled by the leaders are vital, because this determines the success of the operating system. If you want service workers to build relationships with the "heart and head," then you have to engage with their own unique talents, aspirations, and needs. No one does this better than Lloyd Daser.

I asked Daser how he builds the connections between leaders and their direct reports. He has a powerful mindset and approach in this regard:

"If a leader treats each of his/her reports much like one of his/her own children, providing the same guidance, support, and unconditional love (including tough love), they would be a much better leader (unless they are also a lousy parent!). I actually opened a hotel in Malaysia where we built our whole culture around this. We built a birth canal where I 'gave birth' to all of my executive team, who in turn gave birth to their managers, and down the line ... complete with birth certificates. It was certainly an ice breaker for new employees (especially as their new boss screamed in obvious birthing discomfort as they made their way through the birth canal), but it really helped instill family values in our team in a country where the family structure and support system were very strong. I was affectionately known as Grandpa (as opposed to Mr. Daser) by all of our staff, and our relationships with each other very much resembled parenting in all we did."

In terms of leading from the front in building relationships with customers, Lloyd continues, "At the Pan Pacific Kuala Lumpur International Airport hotel, I also had my cellphone programmed and labelled on a speed dial button on the guestroom phone. All guests had direct access to me 24/7 (as they would if they were staying in my home). My life was miserable for six months, but as we worked through their issues and the employees knew that every guest had unfettered access to me, they quickly learned what my hot buttons were and what was important. It sent a great message and built many lasting relationships with our customers, because they knew we stood behind what we promised, and they valued direct access to the GM, because they knew any issues would be resolved. By the end of my tenure there, I think I received more calls from guests extolling the virtues of our hotel and associates than anything else."

This is a great example of how to be a servant leader.

Building mindset

Ensuring employees are always in the right mindset is a key task for leaders. The day that employees slip back into what is best for them rather than best for the customer is a very bad day for the organization. This usually happens when leaders lose their way and focus on growth and profitability or become arrogant through success. There is no better example than Starbucks, when after its runaway success from 1992 to 2006, the company stumbled and nearly went bankrupt. As Howard Schultz, founder and CEO of Starbucks, says, "We had lost sight of our shared purpose and our guiding principles, in which growth and success began to cover up mistakes, and a disease set into Starbucks. That disease, hubris." A major job of the leader is to create a culture where that hubris toward the customers never sets in.

Lloyds Daser talks about how he creates this mindset. "When I opened the Pan Pacific Glenmarie Resort, I bought a life-sized wooden carving of a golfer and named him Vic (very important customer). We put him in our cafeteria and built our culture around it. Everything we did focused on Vic. When someone made a mistake, I simply had to ask them, 'What would Vic think?' If they had a question or needed guidance, I would simply ask them, 'What would Vic do/say?' It made them reflect and they generally came up with the appropriate response on their own." He continued, "When I was at the Pan Pacific Vancouver as front office manager, I set up the Captains Club. We took a picture of any guest who had been with us three times and built a Plexiglas grid in the back corridor where we posted these pictures. We would move their pictures to an 'arriving today/ in-house/checking out' section so the front desk team (and anyone else passing by) would know who was arriving, in-house, or leaving. Guests were constantly amazed how staff members, even new ones whom they had never met before, were able to recognize them by name."

These examples are two ways to keep the mindset of the employee going. In chapter 9, we will explore how Amazon and Ritz-Carlton also use similar approaches to keep the employees' mindset going. These interventions are critical because during busy times when employees are exhausted, these methods can remind an employee why they are there and what the purpose of the company is.

Building relationships through embracing mistakes

As we will discover in the next chapter, many relationships are built by handling mistakes well. Ignoring service errors or becoming defensive when things go wrong (even if the customer has caused the problem) is a great way to destroy trust in the blink of an eye. Conversely, you can build even *stronger* relationships when complaints occur.

As Daser offers, "I think some of the best and strongest relationship we built with customers over the years here in Whistler, and at other hotels I have run, is through service recovery. We screw up in some small (or often not so small) way, and the manner in which you treat the situation in making it right in the customer's eyes can earn you a customer for life. Again, it is about establishing a connection or a bond with your guest."

Building relationships within the community: Adopting the Whistler Experience

Lloyd Daser and his team are also proactive and involve themselves in growing the Whistler Experience within the community (see chapter 3 on the Whistler Experience). Pan Pacific, being an internationally branded hotel, has its own brand vision, purpose, and values. But because it wanted to play a role in driving the community forward, it ensured that it integrated the Whistler Experience concepts (3RS and TOFU, for example) within its own brand vision, purpose, and values, to align its culture and understanding with that of Whistler.

This shows great leadership at the resort level, and Lloyd Daser himself sits on the Whistler Chamber of Commerce board. This is critical because in order to provide great experiences to the customer, you must realize you are one part of an ecosystem and many others are delivering part of that experience too. By Daser and his team adopting the Whistler Experience, they are creating consistency and momentum within the larger community. This leadership has meant that others have followed because of them.

Building the emotional connection

At the end of the day, relationships are built through an emotional connection with the customer. As Daser states, "All associates are empowered with one objective in mind, to make sure the customer has a memorable vacation. It is important to note that building relationships is not just a general manager or director of sales function or responsibility." Perhaps it is the leader's responsibility to create an internal culture that empowers and encourages this, but Daser believes it must be everyone's responsibility, including his.

He adds, "To create responsibility, associates are empowered to spend up to $100 on any guest, at any time, to 'make a guest's day.' Good businesses are reliable and responsive, but great businesses excel at building relationships. This is largely achieved by being connected with your guests and doing or providing something that is unexpected, that leaves a lasting connection or memory with the customer."

He continues, "Relationship building starts from the moment a guest calls to make a reservation. All associates take bookings (not just the reservations department) and take ownership of the guest and reservation (TOFU). Pre-arrival interactions offer assistance with booking activities, answering questions, and helping guests plan their itinerary and vacation."

When in-house, associates are encouraged to interact with the guests at every opportunity, search out and look for opportunities to build relationships, and respond to them. As Daser says, "You have to listen with intent to your customer. Things like recognizing birthdays and anniversaries are easy, but it is much more than this. The hotel hosts an *après* hour daily during ski season where the management team, including me, provides the service and interacts with their guests, builds relationships and looks for opportunities to connect." If you want employees to build strong relationships, lead from the front and they will mirror your behaviour.

The hotel has so many examples of what an empowered workforce can achieve. One anecdote Daser told me highlights the ownership taken by employees at Pan Pacific Whistler: "This story involves a family who had been visiting for a week and unfortunately was stricken with illness for most of their stay. They had one day left of their vacation and were excited about finally getting out for a day of skiing. They were asking the front desk about what time to get up due to the queues on a weekend morning, especially given the forecast was for fresh snow overnight and blue skies in the morning. The guest service agent arranged Fresh Track tickets [early access to ski lifts with free breakfast on the mountain] on behalf of the hotel. Included was a personal note that told them we were happy they were feeling better, and for them to go up ahead of the mountain opening, have breakfast on the top of the mountain, and get in a couple of runs in the morning before any of the regular pass holders reached the top." Imagine the relationship this exemplary service built.

By leading through values and cultural norms, Daser shows us how strong relationships can be built without much need for gimmicks, customer databases, and employee of the month awards. By leading from the front (or, in this case, within the community) and building strong relationships with the employees themselves, firms know that employees will work hard to always build the emotional connection with the customers and even recover from mistakes when things go wrong, without anyone needing to micro-manage them. Without anyone breathing down their necks, they can bring their best to work and show the customers they *really* are at the centre of everything that they do.

3. Go first

The final way to build strong relationship is to go first. This means to do things for customers, and each other, with the expectation of nothing in return. This approach has a potent effect on building relationships.[19]

This approach, of course, is nothing new. Mencius, a Chinese philosopher and a principal interpreter of Confucianism, said many thousands of years ago, "Try your best to treat others as you would wish to be treated yourself, and you will find that this is the shortest way to benevolence."[20] This is the Golden Rule, which is present in many traditions.

To be clear, I do not prescribe to the science of reciprocity: many researchers espouse the idea that you do something for customers in the expectation that you will get something in return.[21] The premise of this book is to "go first" with customers and expect nothing in return—except to build a strong relationship. The research shows that going first changes much in a service context.

The seminal work in this area was undertaken by Adam Grant, whose book *Give and Take* is a modern classic. Grant found there are three types of people who work in organizations.[22]

1. **Givers:** "I'm happy to share my time and energy with those who can benefit." These employees prefer to give more than they get, focus on and act in the interest of others, and help customers without expecting anything in return.

2. **Takers:** "If I don't look out for myself, no one else will." They put their own interests ahead of others' and help others strategically only when the benefits to themselves outweigh the costs. They believe that the world is a competitive, dog-eat-dog place and this is their approach to customers too.

3. **Matchers:** "I'll do it if I'm pretty sure I will get something in return." They strive to preserve an equal balance of giving and getting. This is the reciprocity approach, and it operates on the principle of fairness. They build relationships by an even exchange of favours.

First, by helping other people, givers are exposed to new domains and new problems. Over time, this can accrue to become a formidable cross-disciplinary knowledge advantage.[23] This squares very nicely with Ericsson's purposeful practice approach. Second, givers are the most successful *and* least successful people. As Grant says, "Givers are overrepresented at the top, as well as the bottom, of most success metrics."[24] Givers are overrepresented at the bottom because by putting other people first, they often put themselves at risk for burning out or being exploited by takers. But Grant also found that givers are overrepresented at the top. Grant states, "I found that in sales, the most productive sales people are actually those who put their customers' interests first. A lot of that comes from the trust and the goodwill that they have built, but also the reputations that they create."[25]

What Grant finds is that successful givers are still high on self-interest. They are employees who take determined action to achieve their own ambitious goals while routinely contributing to the success of customers. Yes, we need to build strong relationships, and going first enables us to do that more than other method, but we still need to ensure that by going first we don't stop serving our own customers, being efficient, and using organizational resources carefully. What

Grant is saying is that we shouldn't stop doing our own job effectively just because we are helping others.

Research shows that when you go first, it is most successful if what you do is unexpected, personalized, and meaningful.[26] The Pan Pacific employee giving Fresh Tracks tickets to the family is a great example of this. The gesture was personalized as the customer had mentioned they wanted to go up the ski lifts early, it was meaningful in that it was useful to the customer and had economic value, and it was certainly unexpected.

"Going first" is limited only by your ingenuity. It could simply be a text message to a business customer congratulating them on an amazing contract they have just won, but the research is clear—it will have a more profound effect on the relationship than you will ever imagine, as long as you do it for the right reasons: to sincerely build meaningful connections with your customers.

Dark side of relationships

But as I noted above, for every yin there is a yang. Even going first can sometimes make employees unsuccessful.

My research with Peter Danaher, a professor at the University of Melbourne,[27] showed the impact of having a personal banker manager assigned to you. The strength of the relationship the customer had with the personal banker was surprisingly strong in terms of its impact on customer loyalty. However, what we discovered surprised us: the negative effects were stronger than the positive effects.

In summary, what we find is that a relationship rated as "excellent" will raise overall customer satisfaction and loyalty more than if such a relationship was not in place—no surprise there.

However, a relationship rated as "poor" results in lower overall satisfaction and loyalty among customers compared to those who do not have a personal banker. This was a surprise for the banks that we worked with on this project because they thought that having a personal banker could only be a good thing and certainly not a bad strategy. Moreover, the effects are asymmetric, with negative effects being bigger in magnitude than positive effects.[28]

For example, what we discovered was that, on average, customers who had no personal banker at all rated their likelihood to recommend their bank 3.56 (on a one to five scale). A customer who rated their personal banker as "poor," on average, rated their likelihood to recommend their bank at 2.33—which is 1.23 points lower than those with no personal banker. In contrast, customers who rated their personal banker as "excellent" indicated their likelihood to recommend the bank at 4.27—only 0.71 points higher than those with no personal banker.

This research has an important lesson: don't overpromise on the relationship dimension. Build relationships where it makes sense (i.e., not necessarily with all customers) and work hard, like Joe Girard, to always win the customers over. Never take them for granted.

This asymmetric finding surprised the banks we worked with, and they changed their strategies greatly based on our findings.

RANDOM STORY:
Building Relationships Through Reading

I AM GUESSING you purchased this book because you love reading, and I applaud you for that. It is hard to estimate how much I have learned from reading books. My excitement to read about a new idea or way of thinking is sometimes breathtaking.

Books define our lives so much. Can you recall your favourite childhood book? Or a preferred book you recall reading to your child? I bet you smile when you settle on your most beloved one. The one I enjoyed reading to my kids the most when they were young was *The Shining* by Stephen King. They loved it, and then we watched the movie together. Gripping!

My point is—please keep reading to further build your brand and to learn how to build even stronger relationships with customers.

In the spirit that you always carry on reading, especially when things aren't going your way and the whirlwind has taken over, here are my top eight organization/business/service books of all time. I estimate I have read more than 500 books in these categories, so there are many I considered but rejected. Many of these top eight books I've mentioned elsewhere already, but here they are together.

Peak by Anders Ericsson and Robert Pool
Mindset by Carol Dweck
Influence by Robert B. Cialdini
Thinking, Fast and Slow by Daniel Kahneman
Drive by Daniel Pink
Good Strategy/Bad Strategy by Richard Rumelt
Discovering the Soul of Service by Leonard Berry
The 4 Disciplines of Execution by Chris McChesney, Sean Covey, and Jim Huling

Just to underscore the importance of books, whenever I teach the final class in an undergraduate course, I bring in hard copies of four or five books that we have discussed in the course, so students can see them and flip through them. Just to add a random twist, I always include an old copy of *Conception, Pregnancy and Birth* as one of my recommendations. For some bizarre reason, we bought this book when we were about to have our first child... The opening subject of the book was redundant by then.

Beyond the cheap laugh I get when I introduce this book, the surprising part is that quite a few students come up at the end of the class and look at this book as much as the others.

Happy reading, whatever book you chose!

Recap

Relationship building is about the emotional and empathetic side of service. For example, making customers laugh, complimenting them, and connecting with them through great conversation.

While it might not be as important as reliability or responsiveness in getting customers to rebuy and refer, building relationships is the great differentiator. So many companies are reliable and responsive, but how many do all three consistently? Very, very few.

You can be one of those few.

7

Power of Problem Handling

"**I** SEE WE LOST a few passengers," said Rory to Winton as they left Kaikoura after a whale-watching trip.

"Yes, sadly they were not having fun and others were not enjoying their company either. I think they expected a different kind of trip. These things happen from time to time," said Winton. "The most important thing is to deal with it as soon as you notice, rather than letting it fester—it only gets worse. But everyone seems happier now and they got a full refund."

Rory nodded in agreement.

"Some passengers complained about you as well," said Winton.

"What?!" said Rory.

"Yes, they said your jokes are poor and your dancing is verging on the ridiculous." Winton roared with laughter.

"Fair enough," said Rory. "I agree. But can I please stay on the bus?"

"Sure," said Winton. "But definitely cut out the dancing."

All drivers on the Kiwi Experience are empowered to make decisions for themselves without having to go to managers. This makes sense given the many responsibilities the drivers have. Many issues can arise on a trip like this and drivers have to be ready to deal with them.

In particular, the drivers are trained and empowered to notice any passengers on the bus who might be affecting the quality of the service other passengers are receiving, and are permitted to take appropriate action. For example, in extreme cases, a driver may ask certain passengers to leave the bus and offer a full refund to encourage them to do so. Kiwi Experience has realized that if certain people undermine the enjoyment of a significant proportion of other customers, it is important to remove them from the bus.

Kiwi Experience sometimes has issues with backpackers who want a less action-packed, quieter experience on the bus. These passengers don't like the fast-paced nature of the trip. The passengers are often coached as to whether they are better off using other transport. Solving these problems quickly before anyone complains shows how careful KE is in managing everyone's experience.

Proactively dealing with problems before they become major issues is a critical moment in service situations.

Problem solving *is* relationship building

So here we are, the final moment of power! Sadly, it's about failure. Not a very positive way to wrap up the moments of power, it seems, but the reality is this is one of the most positive things you can do when delivering service. The Pan Pacific case highlighted how handling problems well can help to build positive relationships.

Keep in mind that solving problems is less about *fixing* and more about a chance to develop service excellence by building a relationship with the customer. Any time a customer shares a problem with us, they've gotten it off their chest and we have the opportunity to resolve it. Because after all, people love sharing their problems with others who are sitting on the edge of their seats listening.

This chapter has two dimensions. First, problems caused by the organization, which is the majority of problems. Second, problems that customers cause. Toward the end of this chapter, we'll explore how customers cause about a third of all failures that happen *inside* organizations.[1] As such, we have to be ready to deal with customer failures as well as organizational failures.

I call this chapter "problem handling" and not "complaint handling" because if organizations are clever they can spot a problem before a customer complains. For example, let's say you're sitting in a restaurant waiting for your meal, and you look at your watch because the main course is taking a long time. Then the server comes out and says, "I'm really sorry, but the first time we made your entrée, it wasn't quite right so we're doing it again. I would like to get you a complimentary drink while you are waiting. What would you like?" Before you complained, or even thought about complaining, the server had already identified and tried to solve the problem.

Three parts of problem handling

First, we will consider the research about what happens when a problem occurs and the impact of the resolution. Second, we will examine the idea that two key opportunities emerge from problem handling.[2] Third, and most importantly, we're going to look at how to solve customers' problems. There is extensive research on how you can scientifically and successfully manage and resolve customer complaints. I will present the research that has been done over a number of years on problem handling, including how to prevent and resolve customer failures.

The impact of problem handling

Obviously, handling problems could be considered under the power of expertise (experts handling problems well, which builds trust and credibility) or power of relationships (handling problems effectively strengthens the positive connection between the customer and employee/organization). However, the effect of the power of problem handling is so dramatic that, when it occurs, it is the most impactful moment of all.

The research on handling customer problems, for some reason, is extensive and detailed. I don't really understand why (is it because researching customer complaints is entertaining?), but since 2013 more than 800 papers have been written with "service recovery" in the title. (Service recovery is academic speak for recovering from service problems.) In contrast, the research undertaken concerning coaching employees has spawned only twenty-eight papers in the same timeframe. Clearly, we need to take advantage of this comprehensive research on handling and recovering from problems in the service context.

The area of research that requires us to pay closest attention to problem handling is the impact of handling problems effectively versus ineffectively. The research unequivocally shows that there is an incredible swing between the two outcomes. A group of researchers studied 12,000 customers across a number of service organizations worldwide.[3] Close to 10,000 of the 12,000 customers surveyed didn't have any problems with an organization within the last six months (see column 1 in table 7.1). This group is our control group.

Of these customers, 27 percent were "actively engaged" (extremely loyal customers), 32 percent were "engaged" (loyal), 28 percent were "disengaged" (probably looking for alternatives), and 13 percent were "actively disengaged" (they are probably criticizing the company at every opportunity).

Table 7.1: Effect of problem handling on customer satisfaction

	1. No Problem Last 6 months (n=9951)	2. Had a problem last 6 months (n=1995)	2a. Had a problem but "very satisfied" with how handled (n=421)	2b. Had a problem but not very satisfied with how handled (n=1391)
Actively Engaged	27%	13%	29%	7%
Engaged	32%	24%	36%	21%
Disengaged	28%	30%	24%	32%
Actively Disengaged	13%	33%	11%	40%

If the customers had experienced a problem with the organization (column 2), that picture was very different. There were 20 percent more "actively disengaged" customers and 32 percent fewer "engaged" or "actively engaged" customers in contrast to those customers who have never had a problem. The key managerial takeaway is that firms should avoid problems at all cost, as problems have a huge impact on customer engagement. These results are probably not a surprise.

However, this research can split out those customers who, after a problem had occurred, had a good experience with the problem handling (column 2a) versus those who did not have a good experience with the problem handling (column 2b).

I'd like to highlight the difference in all engagement levels between those customers who are "very satisfied" with the problem handling versus those for whom it was not handled as well. The "actively engaged" number of customers is 29 percent for those where the problem was handled really well versus 7 percent who were less than satisfied. The proportion of "actively disengaged" customers is an amazing 11 percent versus 40 percent. Essentially, those customers who had a problem that wasn't handled very successfully were highly disengaged relative to those customers whose problem was handled very well.

In the moment when you handle the problem well, there's an incredible swing in satisfaction from customers who are "actively disengaged" to those who are "actively engaged." Your managerial recommendation is not necessarily to avoid problems (because there are always going to be problems occurring in service organizations), but to proactively resolve them.

Service recovery paradox

Here's the twist. If you think about those customers who are "very satisfied" with problem handling and compare them to the control group (those customers who didn't have a problem), they're actually a little bit more loyal. In comparison, there is 29 percent versus 27 percent "actively engaged," 11 percent versus 13 percent "actively disengaged," slightly more in the "engaged" category at 36 percent versus 33 percent, and slightly less in the "disengaged" category.

This is called the service recovery paradox[4] because the research shows that often, but not all the time, when you handle a customer complaint expertly, customers may be more loyal than before they had the complaint. Why? Because you've shown how important they are as a customer, and they also believe that not only are you reliable when you get it right the first time, you're also reliable when things go wrong.

I'm not recommending that organizations go out and create problems just so they can solve them really well and create more loyal customers, because that's a dangerous game. "What, there is a giant rat in your sandwich? Leave it to me!"

What I'm actually recommending is that even though we always want to get it right the first time, sometimes things go wrong. But if we are proactive in solving complaints, we may sometimes even be a little bit better off than before the problem occurred.

Please note that you can apply all of the learnings from this chapter to your marriage.

With the impact of complaint handling well established, let's dig a little deeper.

The two key opportunities from problem handling

The research shows that handling problems well presents two opportunities to improve the profitability of service organizations.[5] The first is to resolve the customer problem correctly. The second is to get it right the first time. This is done by classifying the service problem that the customer has identified or you've identified and then integrating that data to improve the overall service system. The idea is that by classifying the service problem, you can be more reliable next time.

There are four steps to handling problems effectively:

1. **Identify the service problem.** Either the customer identifies a problem or, perhaps, you discover it first.

2. **Resolve it.** Recognizing there's a problem, fix it. By resolving customer problems, both your customer and your employees are more satisfied. If an employee is empowered to resolve customers'

problems, then that employee is more engaged in the workplace. They will become more loyal and by doing so they will generate more profitability for the organization.

3. **Classify the service problem.** Integrate all the data you've collected on what causes problems inside your service organization in terms of people, processes, and your physical environment or technology.

4. **Integrate the data and improve the overall service.** By understanding the root causes of problems and failures, we can create a more robust service system that is more reliable. If we don't, we will keep making the same mistakes over and over again, which in the long term will lead to defecting customers and employees. As with resolving customer problems effectively, an employee enjoys working in organizations where the processes work well and are well designed. The customer obviously wants to do business with an organization that is more reliable and, as we've discussed, reliability is the number one driver of success.[6]

How to resolve a problem

There is excellent research on how to handle customer problems effectively: it shows that customers want justice.[7] There are three parts to handling a problem well: a fair outcome, a fair process, and a fair interaction. And you must get all three parts right.

You can't give a fair outcome and a fair process but have a bad attitude toward the customer and make them feel like they're cheating you. Also, you can't give them the right outcome and be friendly about it but then ask them to fill out three forms and ping-pong them around the organization.

Remember, it's all about justice. If you fail at one of those three pieces, the customer will be much less loyal than before they had the problem, but if you get all three right, you may be into the zone of the service recovery paradox.

Figure 7.4 is very straightforward. The *resolution* is what you give the customer to resolve the particular complaint. It's whatever makes sense in that particular scenario; each and every company has to work out what that means specific to its context.

In terms of *efficiency* of the process, this is where TOFU really comes into play. You must take ownership and follow up with customer complaints and problems. When a customer complains and an employee takes ownership of that complaint then resolves it and follows up with the customer to find out whether they were happy with that resolution—wow! That is so rare and extraordinary.

Finally, in terms of the *attitude* of the interaction, this is where honesty, warmth, and friendliness really make the customer feel comfortable about the situation. When customers meet welcoming employees who genuinely want to help, they breathe a huge sigh of relief.

Figure 7.4: Fairness in handling problems

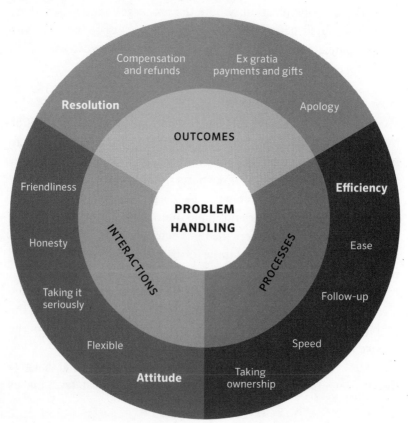

In summary, customers are not looking for you to give them the world. They're looking for you to give a fair outcome to the situation they were faced with, in combination with a fair interaction and a fair process.

If customers feel like they're not getting a fair resolution, process, or interaction, then they will be in that second group of customers: extremely dissatisfied and likely to leave. So make sure that you're ready to spot and listen to problems and, most importantly, ready to resolve them.

Okay, now let's take a moment for another random story.

RANDOM STORY:
The Real Story of Why You Need All Three

ON A FLIGHT on Air New Zealand, I saw a very interesting complaint unfold.

Before I start, I would like to say Air New Zealand is an incredible organization which wins airline of the year almost every year and often competes with Singapore Airlines as the best airline in the world. But, in this case, they didn't do such a great job, which goes to show you no one is perfect.

I was travelling by Air New Zealand in the early 2000s, flying from Auckland to Sydney. It was back in those incredible days when they used to provide you with meals on short flights as well as long ones, whereas now the chance of getting a meal on any two-and-a-half-hour flight is pretty close to zero. I don't think even pilots are allowed to sniff food on short-haul flights. In most domestic flights you also now have to bring your own customer service.

In those heydays, everyone used to get a hot meal on that flight between Auckland and Sydney, but it was also back when they used to say, "Due to previous passenger selection, you may not be able to get the meal that you want." The people at the back of the plane knew that they were going to end up with the piece of rubbery chicken that no one else wanted.

On this flight, I was sitting at the back of the plane. The plane had two seats on each side of the plane and three in the middle. A Norwegian girl was in the other aisle seat in my middle row. (I knew she was Norwegian because I heard her chatting to the person next to me about where she was from, why she was travelling from Auckland to Sydney, etc.)

After about forty-five minutes of the flight, they came down the aisle with the meals and the flight attendant asked the Norwegian girl, "Which meal would you like?" The Norwegian girl said, "I would like the fish." The flight attendant responded, "I'm sorry, we've run out of the fish. Would you like the chicken?" This is where it got interesting. The Norwegian passenger said that she really wanted the fish and wasn't happy with the fact that they only had one choice of the meal left and wondered why they couldn't work out which passengers wanted which meal ahead of time.

No one really wanted to mess with her at all as she was very angry about the whole situation. The flight attendant listened very carefully and then said, "Excuse me, I'll be back in a moment." All of us were kind of holding our breath to see what was going to happen next; the atmosphere in the plane had suddenly turned very tense. But the flight attendant was amazing! She went up to first class and put together a meal from the leftovers. There was smoked salmon, dessert, and a salad.

Everyone breathed a sigh of relief because she'd listened very carefully, gone up, and got a fish meal from first class. However, the flight attendant slammed the tray down on the Norwegian girl's table as a show of defiance. Wait . . . it gets much worse! The Norwegian girl burst into tears because she had just been humiliated in front of all the passengers.

Let's recap in terms of our model. She got a fantastic meal from first class with smoked salmon, dessert, and a salad—great outcome! The process was amazing: The flight attendant was quick, there was no TOFU in the meal, but she certainly took ownership and followed up quickly in this experience.

The fair interaction—um… this is where the flight attendant could use some work.

You must get all three right!

The final piece of research I would like to share with you surrounds the power of one person taking ownership. This research was undertaken by the Technical Assistance Research Program in the U.S.[8] They discovered that satisfaction with the action taken by the employee was very much dependent on how many people they had to speak to before resolving the complaint. If one person took ownership, there was an 80 percent satisfaction rate. But that dropped as soon as ping-ponging started: if a customer has to talk to two people, satisfaction drops to 48 percent; if three or more people are involved, the satisfaction with the action taken is only 23 percent—a great lesson for us all.

CASE STUDY: Ritz-Carlton Hotels

RITZ-CARLTON HOTELS ARE known for their best practices in handling customer complaints.

In terms of resolving complaints, Ritz-Carlton is clear in its training: "Any employee who receives a complaint 'owns' the complaint." In fact, their Service Value 6 (there are twelve) states, "I own and immediately resolve guest problems." Ritz-Carlton states, "Our research indicates that the number of people it takes to resolve a problem directly affects the level of customer engagement. The more people that have to get involved, the lower the engagement score."[9]

In training employees, Ritz-Carlton further states, "React quickly to correct the problem immediately. Follow up with a telephone call within twenty minutes to verify the problem has been resolved to the customers' satisfaction. Do everything you possibly can to never lose a guest." Follow-up is so important; they understand that doing everything they can to never lose the guest is ultimately what customer complaint handling is all about.

A great example of handling a complaint was when a customer stayed in the Ritz-Carlton Hotel in Naples and complained of the low water pressure in the shower. The hotel tested the shower and it wasn't easy to fix, so they moved the customer into another room and gave them passes to the spa, a seventy-five-dollar dining credit, and a late check-out.

The customer wrote in their review that they "could not have expected anything more from the way this negative was reversed into a totally positive experience. This was our fourth stay and we will return to this hotel, one of our favourite hotels anywhere."[10]

MR. BIV is the acronym coined by the Ritz-Carlton to help them in their quest to spot and resolve quality problems. MR. BIV is an efficient, simplified, and easy-to-teach way to look for defects and defective situations, and it can be adopted throughout an entire firm without demanding substantial additional training. It stands for mistakes, rework, breakdowns, inefficiencies, variation in work processes.[11] These are essentially the five errors that can take place inside Ritz-Carlton.

Diana Oreck, vice-president of global learning and the Leadership Center at Ritz-Carlton from 2010 to 2015, said, "MR. BIV has brought us to a point where we honor defects. Our approach to MR. BIV is consistent with the research that shows if you handle a problem quickly, you might get a more loyal guest than if they were no problem at all. While we wish there hadn't been a problem in the first place, we believe there is a need to learn from each imperfection. We want people to report the breakdowns so we can view solutions to remove them from all hotels, not just sweep them under the rug. So Mr. BIV has been a real way to take the stigma out of complaints and helps us reliably track defects to make the necessary corrections."[12]

Ritz-Carlton registers all service breakdowns in the customer database. These incidents and defects are typically shared in the daily lineups the next day (more on the daily lineups in Chapter 9). The additional benefit of maintaining a database of breakdowns is that it allows Ritz-Carlton to be proactive: processes can be modified, training can be delivered, and the service system is more reliable next time.

By making service defects a "good thing," Ritz-Carlton can encourage employees to honestly track shortcomings and take responsibility for quality. In return, Ritz-Carlton leadership receives data that can be used to improve processes and increase reliability. This gives employees more time to build stronger relationships, rather than having to save them.

Ritz-Carlton is so fixated on quality and improving processes (with the help of service breakdowns) that employees are told on the first day that there's nothing more exciting than finding a defect in the system and fixing it. What we know now is that delivering a memorable service experience to the customer can't happen unless we are fixated on being reliable first.

In fact, Ritz-Carlton is so good at this they say they can deliver luxury service "economically." That is how you make money through world-class service.

Customer failures

In many ways, a customer failure can be harder to recover from than a company failure. When a company fails, it's clearly the company's fault and you've likely seen this failure before, so you understand which best practices to use to recover. When a customer fails, all hell can break loose because though it's not the organization's fault, clearly you want to save the relationship. What do you do then? Given the inevitability of this scenario, we'll explore how to handle this situation.

Also, sometimes the customer causes the issue, so they may not complain. They just have a problem they need solved, and they need your help to solve it. Here's a great personal example.

There is a local float plane airline in British Columbia called Harbour Air. They mainly fly between Vancouver and Victoria, but they also do lots of other coastal flights within BC. I was working in Vancouver and I made my way to the six p.m. flight home, the last flight of the day. Well, as it happened the last flight had actually left at 5:30 p.m. and I had forgotten the time it left (I was busy, okay?).

No-shows get charged the full fare because Harbour Air loses out on the seat they could have booked. I know and accept these conditions. However, I have been flying with them for years and it was the first time I'd made this mistake. The next day I called them and explained what happened (again, not a complaint—I knew it was my fault), but it was a problem—they had charged me the fare on my credit card and as a loyal customer, I felt I had a case to make for a refund. So did they, luckily. They saw it from my point of view (and probably saw that I was a regular customer too) and refunded me the amount immediately. This, in turn, has undoubtedly built my relationship with them.

I'm not saying we must always refund the customer or fix the issue when they make a mistake (although we should always do our best to do so), but we should have a plan and consider carefully what to do when this does happen, rather than leaving an employee to work it out for themselves.

One-third of all failures are caused by the customer. Think of an example of a customer forgetting an appointment at the dentist. Should they charge the customer for that? I know you are thinking, "Sure, that's their fault." Now, what if it was you and you'd been going to this dentist for more than ten years and your whole family goes too? Do you still think it is fair?

A great example of the customer failure dilemma is from a premier hotel chain.[13] In this example, the manager highlights that when the hotel is at fault for overbooking they will go "overboard" to accommodate the customer, including even "a free weekend at the hotel with the spouse at some future date."[14] The manager of the hotel continues, "In situations where the traveller is at fault, the solution is left to the discretion of the front desk. If your reservation says you must be there at six p.m. and you turn up at 6:30 p.m. and you have not bothered to inform the hotel that you will be late, then you are at the mercy of the clerk if there are no rooms available. We are mortified when that happens. Remember the goal is to resolve the situation in such a way that people want to come back and stay with us again."[15]

In response to this dilemma, I wrote a paper with Steve Tax and David Bowen and we suggest three things that you need to do to avoid customer failures.[16] First of all, diagnose these failures. Ask questions: When do these failures occur? What causes the most customer failures? Which ones lead to most frustrations with a customer? If you don't understand what causes customer failures, then you can't resolve them. Next, discover the root causes. Customer failure will come from one of four areas. Maybe the process is too complex, or the signs aren't clear; perhaps the website isn't well designed, or the customers don't have the right skills. By understanding the root causes of a customer failure, we can resolve them.

Finally, we need to implement preventative solutions that can stop problems from happening again. An example we discussed was redesigning process to reduce customer confusion. For example, redesign a booking process to ensure customers make the right choices, such as the right meal plan and room on a cruise ship. Use technology to assist the customer, such as sending a text reminder of an appointment or making it easier for customers to cancel appointments. (No one wins when customers forget to cancel appointments they can no longer make.) We can even get customers to help each other; Weight Watchers members attend weekly meetings that involve group discussions and weigh-ins to measure progress. This is an example of how customers stop each other from failing.

Customer failures account for a third of all failures between service firms and customers. If we're not proactive in managing them, then our service process will be a lot more inefficient, making customers and employees unhappy. We should always be on the front foot to prevent them from occurring as much as organizational failures.

Recap

When you solve a problem, you must understand that customers have the highest expectations when things go wrong. You must be ready for the fact that sometimes they've caused the mistake themselves, but that doesn't mean you can brush the problem under the carpet and ignore them.

When it's clear that the organization has caused the problem, customers want justice in terms of the resolution, the process, and the interaction—and you must get all three right.

Problem resolution is also a very rare chance to create loyalty. I really want you to think about that. There aren't many chances in the service context for creating loyalty. Most transactions are straightforward. But suddenly when there is a problem, the customer is on their tiptoes, wondering what the organization is going to do. By handling it well, you show that you're not only the expert in reliability and in getting it right the first time, but also you're an expert in terms of fixing problems.

Like Ritz-Carlton, if you are willing to learn from these defects, then you are continually building a stronger organization. You may even be so much of an expert that you know how to avoid customer failures and you redesign your system so that customers can always be successful too.

Ready for the last letter of FAME? I thought so. Me too. I'm exhausted. Do you fancy a cocktail first?

FAME PART 4
ENDURANCE

OH, HOW IRONIC that the last section in the book is called Endurance. Great you made it this far! I really must commend you on your persistence, resilience, and grit—unless of course you're in my service class and you had no choice but to read this whole book or you would've failed. In that case, I praise you for choosing my class in the first place. Oh, you chose this class because of my Rate My Professors score? Well, let me tell you I wrote most of those reviews. You can't believe anything you read on the internet.

Delivering world-class service is about the long haul: not giving up when you hit a roadblock and not becoming arrogant when you've made it to the top. It's about sustaining service excellence. And so, in this context, service is about endurance. It's about delivering great service when other companies have focused their attention elsewhere. It's about tapping into people's potential and helping them grow every day through coaching (the focus of chapter 8), by sharing the voice of the customer, telling customer stories, and reminding everyone that the customer is at the centre of everything that you do (the focus of chapter 9). Finally, it's about building commitments that enable you to pay attention to the service effort each and every day.

Let's go back to the analogy of running. You could have trained all you want and adopted all the disciplines to help you run a fantastic race, but you still need to run that race and persist when it's easier to quit. You might feel like you're hitting a wall at some point in your journey and like carrying on seems impossible. That's when endurance kicks in.

Endurance means you have prepared for the struggle to cross the finish line. Great service organization don't find delivering service in difficult situations any more fun or easier than the good companies. But the difference is that the great companies have more faith; they have an unshakable belief in what they are doing and they desire the outcomes of great service more than the good companies. This means they are willing to endure. Successful service companies do what less successful service companies are simply not willing to do—not because it comes easier to them, but because they want it more. This means they understand the importance of endurance and organize for it. This chapter is about that organization.

So, what do successful companies do in the service area that the less successful ones don't do?

1. Great service companies endure by coaching their employees to deliver great service continually. In particular, they take an athletic approach to coaching. They don't have comfortable one-on-one conversations with employees about how they can improve. They observe them, collect data on their performance, and give feedback—which inspires employees and helps them grow—so service delivery is always improving. When you are coached to grow your service expertise, you endure far more than an employee who isn't.

2. Great service companies endure by building commitments. They meet regularly to talk about service so they can continually think about ways to improve the customer experience. These commitments mean that they never stop thinking about service, and that alone can make all the difference in the world.

3. Great service companies endure by sharing the voice of the customer. They relate the customers' stories with their employees so that they can keep the importance of the customer service journey alive. Telling stories of how their service makes a difference in the customers' lives, sharing customer compliments, and highlighting

the progress that they're making from the customer's point of view enables them to get out of bed just a little bit quicker every morning to carry on the service journey.

These three interventions are the subjects of the last two swash-buckling chapters.

8

Coaching

"**I**'M GOING TO leave the bus here in Queenstown," stated Rory to Winton. "A group of us are going to stay here for a few weeks and take in the amazing scenery. I've met some great people on the bus and we have decided to hang out together."

"Great idea," said Winton. "Make sure you book yourself on the bus; one comes through here every day in the summer."

"Thanks for the most incredible time, Winton," added Rory with a lump in his throat. "Maybe you'll be driving the next bus we catch."

"I hope not," said Winton. "There are many great drivers—it will be good for you to meet another one."

One thing that the management of Kiwi Experience constantly strives for is to increase the frequency of its bus services. They have realized that the more often the buses operate, the more flexible their service becomes. This increases its attractiveness to potential customers.

Market research has shown that value for money is the third most important aspect of the KE trip. The price of the tickets, the activities offered, and the flexibility and the quality of the service prompt many backpackers to feel that they are obtaining value from KE. To date, the company has managed to maintain this perception, and it is one of the fundamental reasons for its success.

However, KE does not intend to stall. Neil Geddes knows that in order to stay ahead of the competition, the company must always improve its service offering. As he said, "We are our own biggest threat, being seen as mainstream or not leading edge, or by becoming a service that is perceived as not being for independent travellers. We must continually move with the market to ensure we offer the best possible experience for our customers."

Being successful means always doing whatever you can to stay ahead of the game. In this respect, it's all about endurance. Sustaining excellence with customers and avoiding hubris—as Neil Geddes says, we are often our own worst enemy and to avoid this we must build practices that stop complacency and arrogance from setting in.

Coaching is the first step.

Coaching

There is a symbiotic relationship between customer service and coaching. The science of service, which is built around the 3Rs of reliability, responsiveness, and relationships, gives you a behavioural framework in which to educate employees on how to deliver great service.

Having a service framework built on science does not mean that employees will execute great service every day. How do you ensure employees are acting on the 3Rs and working hard to improve their skills in these three areas? The secret behind executing great service every day is taking a constant athletic approach to coaching.

Begin by observing employees in their service role while demonstrating the customer skills you would like the employee to deliver, and identify growth opportunities for the employee. Then commit the employee to practice those identified skills. This approach will advance their *technical* service skills. The athletic approach to coaching also grows their *mental* skills by showing that you believe in the coachee and their growth, while creating challenging goals and giving them regular feedback as they progress toward those goals.

Finally, the athletic approach to coaching means you are helping employees have *energy* when they work on the front line. This means helping front-line employees to be safe at work, helping to manage the stress that comes with working on the front line, and also helping them manage their wellness (by reminding them of employee health benefits, for example).

When you take this approach to coaching front-line employees, it means they develop mastery, focus, and energy. They will then be much more likely to deliver great service as they have become (or are becoming) service *experts*. Figure 8.1 offers a summary of this approach.

Figure 8.1: Athletic approach to customer service coaching

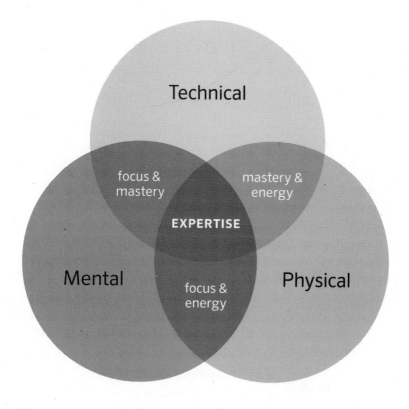

You need both a strong behavioural framework *and* an athletic approach to coaching. If you coach regularly but don't have a

behavioural framework—in this case, the 3Rs—then what content will you coach with? What's in your playbook that enables you to spot what employees are doing well and where they can improve? The 3Rs gives you coaching content and a checklist to specifically recognize high performance and carefully identify areas for even higher levels of service performance.

Behavioural framework + athletic approach to coaching = Sustained service excellence

By executing both of these parts, you can set yourself apart from other organizations that do only one or, in many cases, neither. In this way, you can determine your own service FAME.

Let's explore the three parts to an athletic approach to service in more detail. (You hoped I wasn't going to say that, didn't you?)

Building technical skills

Observation

The best customer service coaching sessions use observationally based data. In the best case scenario, although not always possible, this necessitates the coach witness the employee in their service role.

When I say *observe*, I use the word in its broadest sense. That is, the observation could be hearing an employee serve a customer on the phone. It could be witnessing a customer interaction in an online chat room by reading the transcript. These techniques qualify as objective observational data. Further, the coach does not have to collect the data themselves. Providing the data is credible and relevant, it can come from another source. For example, we can do mystery shops and use the data from the shopper for the coaching sessions.

Demonstration

Another effective way for a coach to grow someone's technical skills is by demonstrating the skill that they would like the employee to acquire. Athletic coaches usually demonstrate their knowledge by acting out or simulating the desired skill. Leading by example through demonstration is a good way for the coachee to model behaviour after the coach. In doing so, the coach could demonstrate effective behaviour directly to the coachee.

A team leader demonstrating how to handle a frustrated customer, a retail store manager demonstrating how an employee can build rapport with a customer in a face-to-face context, or a sales manager demonstrating to another salesperson how to do a needs analysis with a customer are three examples of how demonstration can play out in a service context. These demonstrations also lend credibility to the leader who displays the skill they are trying to teach. Remember, great athletic coaches model skills to their athletes.

Another effective technique is *upward coaching*, where a service employee coaches this team leader, for example, so that the team leader not only demonstrates the skill they would like the employee to acquire but also receives feedback on improving that skill, if appropriate. Upward coaching allows the leader to show vulnerability and that they are willing to put their integrity on the line and be coached as well. This is an excellent modelling strategy.

Practice

Another way to grow a technical skill in a service context is to allocate practice time for the employee.

In an organizational context, this requires the coach to ensure that the employee commits to a particular work plan at the end of the coaching session and determine how they will practice that particular skill before the next coaching session. Without this commitment to practice at the end of the coaching session, there is unlikely to be any technical change in the employee's skills.

One way of practicing off-line is through role play: acting out a technique with an expert, team leader, or another employee, so that their practice can be more deliberate. In this way, they practice and get feedback without involving a customer.

Obviously, employees cannot endlessly take time away from work to practice deliberately. Most athletes spend much of their time in practice and little time performing. Service employees, however, have to spend most of their time working for an internal or external customer. Much of this practice time, then, needs to happen in real time (i.e., when the employees are actually serving customers). This means you need to create a safe environment for them to practice skills and encourage them to take risks, but manage these risks carefully.

No athlete—not even an amateur—would consider performing without practice. Yet organizations rarely allow their employees hands-on practice, role playing, or simulations. This practice time could well be the difference that moves you from good to great.

High-quality and timely feedback

Another way of growing someone's technical skills is by offering feedback—the coach identifies if the coachee is on the path to acquiring a particular service skill or if changes still need to be made.

In most service roles, employee feedback occurs very irregularly (e.g., in the annual performance review or without context). This feedback is neither timely nor useful.

High-quality feedback is based on systematically identifying opportunities to give regular feedback to employees, so they know they are making progress or they need to make changes to build further progress. Feedback must be provided at the earliest opportunity so the employee feels like they are on the right track. In these instances, consistent—versus irregular—coaching sessions make all the difference in the world. This feedback should also be performance-based and zero in on specific skills—it's about raising their game so they execute at a higher level.

The list below summarizes the different coaching tactics for developing technical skills based on using an athletic approach to coaching in organizations.

Five coaching tactics for growing technical skills

1. Coach observes employee performing in their role.
2. Coach demonstrates new skills or techniques.
3. Coach gives regular time to coachee to practice new skills.

4. Coach gives feedback at the earliest opportunity to the coachee, rather than waiting for formal job evaluations.
5. Coach gives valuable performance feedback, so coachee grows their service abilities.

Building mental skills

The second dimension of athletic coaching that needs to be developed in most organizations concerns service employees' mental skills. Coaches use their expertise to assist employees in developing their ability to be focused, determined, committed, and confident in their service roles. The development of psychological skills requires a systematic coaching program designed to use the employee's strengths, while also addressing weaknesses, to keep the focus on achieving targeted goals, even in the face of unexpected challenges (which all organizations face).

We will now examine three areas of mental skill training—setting goals, inspiring the coachee by showing you believe in them, and helping the coachee improve their mental focus.

Goal setting

Goal setting is one of the most influential theories of employee motivation. In a survey of organizational behaviour scholars, it has been rated as *the* most important theory (out of seventy-three theories).[1] The theory has been supported by more than 1,000 studies with employees ranging from blue-collar workers to research-and-development employees, and there is robust support that setting goals is connected to employee performance developments.[2] The theory is simple: when a coach helps an employee to set goals, the employee will raise their performance in contrast to employees who don't have a coach urging them to set goals.

In order to motivate employees, goals should be SMART: specific, measurable, achievable, relevant, and time-bound. Employees will not be motivated by having any old goal. SMART goals motivate coachees because they energize behaviour, give it direction, provide a challenge, force employees to think outside the box, and devise new and novel methods of performing. The Lululemon case study, below, is a wonderful example of this.

Effective goals are specific and measurable because if they aren't, how would you know whether you have reached the goal? Without specific goals, a wide variance of performance levels could potentially be acceptable.

Effective goals are also relevant and time-bound. Employees see how these goals will develop them in ways they think are meaningful and are connected to their service goals. Also, effective goals contain a statement regarding when the proposed goal will be reached. For example, "increasing service scores in this region by 8 percent by end of the next fiscal year" gives employees a sense of time urgency. Again, the role of the coach is to ensure that the goals the employees are setting are in line with all of the above criteria. Coaches need to become experts at helping employees set goals, because the difference they make is undeniable.

There are two further conditions that contribute to goal effectiveness, once goals have been set.[3] First, the coachee must receive feedback on their progress toward their SMART goals. Providing employees with quantitative figures about growing customer satisfaction or other metrics is useful for feedback purposes. Also, the coach may be able to spot progress in particular areas that relate to the goals in the continual coaching sessions and provide feedback that identifies, qualitatively, that they are growing and improving in their service role.

Second, the employee must commit to the goals that have been set. As a testament to the importance of goal commitment, Microsoft actually calls employee goals "commitments."[4] Goal commitment refers to the degree to which a person is dedicated to reaching the goal. Research shows that when individuals have a supportive and trust-based relationship with the coach, goal commitment tends to be higher. Similarly, when the coach ensures that the coachee participates fully in the goal setting process, the coach is more likely to be committed too.[5]

In summary, goal setting, providing feedback on goal progress, and obtaining goal commitment from the coachee are key skills the coach must master to ensure the employee has focused goals that steer them to success within the organization.

The coach encourages, believes, and connects

One of the amazing things coaches can do for employees is believe in them. Again and again, I hear in the seminars I teach that the best coaches are the ones who believe in the people they coach. When this happens, employees are far more inspired to achieve their goals and grow in their respective fields, whether in sports or in an organizational context. Believing in the coachee is the second way, after setting meaningful goals, to drive the mental skills of the employee.

When a coach believes in us, we entertain possibilities that stretch the limits of our own thinking. Part of this involves building the coachee up rather than knocking them down—great coaches always build self-esteem rather than undermine it.

A coach who is authentic, who always turns up to coaching sessions, and who demonstrates that they have the employee's best interests at heart are indeed the best coaches, regardless of how long they have been coaching. These qualities are far better than an experienced coach who has lost interest in their coachees.

The coach provides strategies to improve the coachee's mental focus

Finally, a good coach can help the coachee grow mentally by providing explicit strategies to improve the coachee's focus, particularly in high-stakes situations. Some of the most successful strategies that athletes use are visualization and self-talk.

Visualization is using imagery to see the outcomes you want to occur and learning to deal with them before they arise.[6] Effective imagery is used to increase coachee motivation and attention control while decreasing performance anxiety.[7] Bruce Peltier reported on lessons from athletic coaches and concludes, "Virtually all successful athletic coaches use covert imagery rehearsal, or visualization."[8]

Self-talk involves repeating mood-triggering words and positive self-statements to gain concentration.[9] Another mental skill involves reframing self-talk by turning negatives into positives.[10] Obviously, employees will not use self-talk all the time, but in a high-stakes situation like a tough customer negotiation, then self-talk may be useful.

Five coaching tactics for growing mental skills

1. The coach helps the coachee set goals.
2. The coach helps the coachee evaluate goals and progress through feedback.
3. The coach obtains goal commitment from the coachee.
4. The coach encourages, believes, and connects with the coachee.
5. The coach provides strategies to improve the coachee's mental focus.

Building physical skills

The final dimension of adopting an athletic approach is helping to ensure service employees have energy at work. While some organizations have taken this approach very seriously, many more do not see it as part of their role as an employer.

Service coaches who ignore the physical side of coaching are missing an opportunity for a complete approach. It seems clear that an employee who has energy at work will be happier, higher performing, and better able to serve the customer.

Many researchers suggest that energy is an employee's most important resource and fundamental to high performance.[11] Put simply, an employee who has poor work–life balance, or a service employee who has poor health due to a lack of education and coaching, is an employee who is unlikely to give their best at work.

All Whole Foods employees, for example, receive a 20 percent discount on store purchases, but they can get discounts of up to 30 percent if they meet certain criteria for blood pressure, cholesterol, smoking status, and body-mass-index screenings. An internal company website allows employees to track their eating habits. Other health benefits vary from region to region based on employee requests and local interests, but they include massage therapy and yoga. Plus, all employees are eligible for six-week sabbaticals for every 6,000 hours of service. All of this adds up to a company that is focused on the energy levels of an employee.

Coaching for physical skills

Given that we see some organizations interested in promoting physical fitness and health while others are reluctant to get involved in this activity, the question is how should coaches go about coaching people so they are safe, healthy, and have energy at work?

This is where the notion of the *head coach* becomes important. The best role you can often play is head coach, where you actually may coach from time to time but more often will use other people to help you coach. You can use their different perspectives to fill in some of the blanks for the coachee and for you as the head coach. This head coach analogy means that you, as the coach, don't have to do everything for the employee.

It is unlikely that most people who are coaching in a service context have been trained to offer competent health advice. Also, think about how uncomfortable that would be on a one-to-one basis. ("Excuse me, but where do you think that piece of chocolate cake will get you?")

There are a few ways this can work. The first is team-based coaching. In this scenario, a coach provides education and advice to the team as a whole rather than singling out one particular person. The coach might organize health events for the team such as yoga sessions, health seminars by specialists (perhaps to discuss hydration in the workplace or correct posture while sitting), or team-based competitions (e.g., who can walk the most steps in the week), with the winner getting a health-related prize (rather than a thick-crust pepperoni pizza).

Second, as the head coach, you can ensure that any health benefits provided by the organization are shared with the coachees. For example, reminding employees of their health benefits: gym memberships, free annual checkups, and so on. Sharing with employees all the benefits that are available to them is a great way to promote a healthy work environment.

Finally, in the role of head coach, you could point individual employees toward specific health specialists; for example, giving coachees access to physiotherapists, chiropractors, or therapists as appropriate.

A major part of health in the workplace is work–life balance: managing stress as a front-line employee and staying relaxed at work. Again, remember how difficult it is for an athlete to perform if they are burned out. Kiwi Experience, if you recall, evaluates their drivers for burnout at the end of every trip.

While some may think this form of coaching should fall under the *mental skills* of coaching, the reality is that the first signs of stress and burnout are physical signs: an employee has trouble sleeping, their eating habits become erratic, or their health begins to decline, and it manifests in headaches, constant sickness, and other related symptoms, such as chest pains and tense muscles.

The more the coach understands that the physical side of the workplace is important, the more they will educate themselves in this area and provide the right education and advice for the service employee.

The list below shows the five tactics coaches can use to promote physical skills. I believe this is an emerging area in organizations and particularly in service coaching. Those who guide service employees on technical, mental, *and* physical skills are taking coaching a step further by viewing the employee as a complete person. Thinking about everything you can do to help a coachee develop mastery in service.

Five coaching tactics for growing physical skills

1. A good coach improves a coachee's physical fitness.
2. A good coach improves the coachee's ability to stay relaxed and manage stress.
3. A good coach improves the coachee's ability to prevent injuries.
4. A good coach helps the coachee to develop healthy eating habits.
5. A good coach encourages the coachee to stay hydrated.

CASE STUDY: Lululemon

LULULEMON IS A retail athletic brand whose offerings include premium-quality clothing such as pants, tops, shorts, and jackets for fitness activities like running and yoga. In addition to clothing, the company also sells accessories such as bags, socks, and yoga mats. While the company's products mostly target women who aim for a healthy lifestyle while balancing a busy life, the company has expanded its reach by also targeting men and youth.

Despite being a relatively young company, they are valued at more than US$12.5 billion, largely because they created a valuable market offering but also because of the goal setting and feedback approach with employees.

Lululemon identified a target market that wasn't being served and created an incredibly loyal following of customers and employees. Remarkably, they are fourth in the U.S. and second in Canada for sales per square foot within their retail stores (around US$2,000 per square foot on an annualized basis).[12]

The main reason I want to highlight Lululemon is their approach to feedback and goal setting with employees. They truly execute the three parts to the athletic approach to coaching. The company's core is goal setting and their goal-setting toolbox continues to evolve as the company grows. Let's look at how they coach people to be technically, mentally, and physically in their best shape.

Mental

Goal setting is done on a one-year, five-year, and ten-year scale and is broken into categories of personal, professional, and health. Employees usually have two or three goals per category. Employees then break down each ten-year goal so a portion of it can be accomplished in five years, and then how parts of that five-year goal can be accomplished in one year. This makes the ten-year goal not so far out of reach. Performance evaluations are done every six months and aren't necessarily always in relation to goals, though they are reviewed. Co-workers and managers are always holding employees accountable for their goals, as they are always visible in store or around head office. For example, goals are posted on walls around the office and employees in the stores have their visions posted on the "vision board" inside the store, visible to customers, to keep the focus on development at all times.

The main step in setting goals is to write down the "big picture" vision. This is called a "big hairy audacious goal (BHAG)." This is the long-term vision that may take many years to accomplish. From the BHAG, smaller goals can be set that are in line with the big picture. When a BHAG is achieved, a celebration is always a must! This is done for both individual goals as well as goals for the company.

Setting the employee's personal goals and growth starts in the onboarding, which is a full week, where 90 percent of the time is focused on personal development and 10 percent on the company, products, and benefits. This sets the tone for employees' time in the company.

The company also provides many personal development tools and opportunities and really cares about individual goals outside of Lululemon—even if these educational or travel goals means leaving Lululemon. Overall the culture is to support development, learning, and growth with an approach that encourages people to push themselves and get what they want in the company and in life—making it an environment most employees love.

Technical

With clear goals in mind, coaching employees for technical skills becomes an easier task. At Lululemon, employees are called "educators," highlighting the focus on creating expertise. In coaching employees, they focus on explaining the technical elements of each item—as well as fit—to potential customers.

Employees are continually observed and coached on the store floor to provide a better experience for the client. Store leaders spend much time giving feedback to "educators" so they can become even better at educating the customer. This means the customer gets a better experience and the employee can be better at sales. Peers are encouraged to give feedback to each other. This is possible when you have created a safe environment for employees to give and receive feedback.

In summary, educators and managers are constantly holding one another accountable for their goals.

Energy

This coaching culture—as you would expect with a lifestyle brand—extends to health as well. The company invests in their people (free workout classes, seminars, etc.) so they will lead a healthier life, enriched with yoga. They also offer health and wellness benefits (such as extended medical coverage) that are in line with this approach. There are at least three classes every day at head office that employees can take advantage of, ranging from yoga to dance to circuit.

Also, each employee in the company receives a monthly allowance to spend on fitness classes (you can end up attending many classes, depending on what you choose). The management does expect that people take classes, which often take place in a local studio or gym. Lululemon helps support their affiliate studios as well as keeps their employees healthy and fit. The company will often declare a sweat challenge (in store or companywide) where employees are broken into teams or stores. The prizes for winning are always amazing (like dinner at an expensive restaurant or a boat party in New York), which keeps everyone very motivated.

At initial employee training, which lasts a week, there is yoga each morning. In the retail stores, yoga (or some other form of physical activity) also occurs during team sweat sessions and before, during, or after team meetings. Essentially, employees are being paid to practice yoga at work.

Recap

Coaching plays triple duty in elevating your brand. First, every time you coach, you build the relationship between the leader (or peer) and the employee. You are connecting with them, and that alone is invaluable.

Second, the employee becomes more engaged. They are growing and making progress, and every time they experience powerful coaching, their commitment to their work deepens.

Finally, and most importantly, the customer experiences that employee growth through an increase in the quality of service they receive. Brilliant!

9

Building Commitments
and Using the
Customer's Voice

AFTER COACHING, THE next best way to endure in service is to
build commitments that you know will make a difference.

We have come across so many commitments already in the
case studies. Consider Kiwi Experience's debriefing with the driver at
the end of every trip, Jeff Bezos's customer chair, the Commonwealth
Bank's "big five" ideas in the Monday morning sales and service meeting and the after-action review on Fridays, and Whistler Blackcomb's
monthly service meetings that all business heads attend.

Essentially, building commitments hold attention and keep work
progressing. Without these commitments, we slip back into our old
habits and move away from focusing on the customer. Take the coaching section above. You may have the best intentions in the world to
use coaching, but without building commitments to continually coach,
those intentions will evaporate, as the whirlwind takes over and other
urgent (but less important) activities take over the day.

We ensure that we stay focused on our macro service vision by
building micro commitments that inform the everyday. There are

four parts to this: choosing the commitment (less is more), scheduling the commitment (which provides the discipline), knowing the behaviour that drives success (i.e., the best way to execute the commitment), and measurement (identifying progress because of this commitment).

Choosing the commitments

Success with your commitments is all about not over-committing. If you create too many commitments, then you will end up exhausted and distracted. Which commitments will make the biggest difference? Obviously, the service system we identified in chapter 3 should guide the commitments to achieve the service vision, connect with important metrics, and drive HR practices. I believe that the following are the three commitments that every firm should consider.

1. **Continual service meetings.** Like Whistler Blackcomb and Commonwealth Bank did, build a commitment for all teams to meet (even teams that have no external customers). Ritz-Carlton is famous for their daily lineups, their version of the football huddle. A daily lineup is a standing meeting that includes all staff and takes place at the beginning of each shift. The lineups typically take about fifteen minutes and serve as a warm-up, a tune-up, and a catch-up; they have a lasting impact on employee engagement and organizational culture.[1]

   The warm-up refers to ensuring employees are in the right mindset at the beginning of each day. The tune-up refers to picking a service concept to focus on and discuss, and the catch-up refers to communicating an important piece of company news (maybe service scores from last week).

2. **Commitment to coaching.** You should be coaching, and you yourself should be coached. A commitment to continual coaching meetings is crucial. But be warned, it's better to choose not to coach than to choose to it and then do it badly.

Recently, I co-conducted a survey of 700 employees who worked in organizations across North America.[2] We asked the employees where they worked, what kind of coaching they received, how engaged they were at work as an employee, and whether that coaching was part of a formal coaching program or an ad hoc program (if they received any coaching at all). The results surprised us, and they are a fantastic reminder of the power of being coached by a supervisor/leader. Seventy-nine percent of employees in the survey who received moderate to high levels of coaching, based on seventeen different dimensions of coaching,[3] said they were engaged at work. If they received low levels of coaching or no coaching at all, then only 46 percent were engaged at work.

If the employees said they were part of a formal coaching program, however, but were not happy with it (i.e., the leaders said they were going to coach them and then they didn't turn up), then only 34 percent of them were engaged—the lowest engagement of all three groups. The message here is clear: effective coaching drives employee engagement well beyond levels of those who are not receiving adequate levels of coaching. However, it is far better to do no coaching than to promise to do coaching and then not deliver on the promise. That certainly seems to be a recipe for low employee engagement.

This is why sticking to a coaching commitment is critical.

3. **Employee recognition opportunities.** These are non-cheesy significant occasions where exceptional employees are recognized for living out service values. Recall Whistler Blackcomb's monthly events at the prestigious restaurant on the mountain (while still being paid for work), along with their commitment to handing out vouchers on the spot to employees delivering great service in the moment.

   A commitment to meaningful and well-branded employee celebration occasions are amazing ways to highlight how much leaders value service and motivate employees to access these events. The more communication and excitement there is around them, the more employees will aspire to them.

Scheduling the commitment

This is where the habit is really formed. Entering into your calendar the exact time that this commitment will occur changes everything, because it suddenly transforms from being an idea to something you have committed to—as has everyone who was invited and accepted the invitation.

This could be a coaching session, a service meeting, an employee recognition event, or a focus group with customers to understand their current service perception.

So many good intentions disappear because people plan to do them but never get around to executing them. Diarizing these commitments makes them much more likely to happen. Essentially, the idea is to commit to the commitment.

Understand behaviour that drives commitments—streaking!

Once you have scheduled the commitment, you need to understand the best way of executing it.

A great way to start and sustain a service commitment is to create a "streak." No, it's not running naked across a football field during the halftime show. A streak is doing a behaviour intentionally, consistently, and consecutively.[4] In this respect, a streak is an action that is repeated over and over again to create a habit.

As the authors of the book *Goals, Habits, Streaks* write, "A streak is not about accomplishing something amazing in a short period of time."[5] A streak is the smallest, simplest activity that you can do to keep a service commitment going. It is a thing that you do to win a daily, weekly, or monthly game. A streak should be so simple to accomplish daily that you wonder, "Will it really make a difference to my service goals?" Streaking changes the fundamental focus from "I should be doing this thing" to "I wonder how many days or weeks in a row I can do this thing and for how long?"

If you want to be consistent in a commitment with no finish line (the definition of delivering great service), or sustain a behaviour with no time limit, or maintain a standard for your life, start a streak. If you doubt the power of streaks, think of Snapchat streaks—users are obsessed about carrying them on for as long as they can. Let's use the same psychological technique in delivering consistently high levels of service.

Measure the success of commitments

Finally, you need to measure the success of the commitments. Are they making a difference? Is this time well spent? How can we redesign these commitments so they make a bigger impact?

Understanding the progress you are making and learning how to tweak commitments to make them even more effective (or end them, if they are ineffective) makes you more likely to endure. If you start the commitments but do not measure success or collect any kind of feedback, then people may wonder why they are doing them and slowly peter out. People play games when they know the score and, in particular, when they know they are winning. Visibly show the impact of the commitment and it will endure.

Again, think about coaching. If you are measuring whether coaching is driving service performance with employees, whether the employees are enjoying the sessions, and whether you are getting a return on investment, then you are much more likely to be successful with coaching than if you don't measure any of these things. By measuring the success of coaching, you are able to make a decision as to how to improve it or whether you should be building new commitments that may be more effective than coaching.

Using the customer voice

The final way to build endurance is to share the customer voice, so that employees always hear stories of how their service is making a difference. The more customer stories, compliments, and any other useful feedback is passed on to the employee, the more likely it will keep momentum up in terms of how service makes a difference in customers' lives.

One of the biggest problems organizations face is when employees become jaded and forget the importance of making customers feel special and the meaning it has in their work. This can be particularly true at busy times of the day, week, or year. As noted in the Ritz-Carlton daily lineups, they often share customer stories that inspire the employees. At the Commonwealth Bank of Australia, the CEO, Sir Ralph Norris, sent an email to all employees at lunchtime each Friday to let them know what key events were happening and what he was doing each week as CEO. Very cleverly, he also always included a customer compliment about an employee who had delivered fantastic service. This employee then became a superstar for the week as they were recognized for their efforts. More importantly, however, along with the story, the CEO also highlighted the key service principle that was at play in the story (such as TOFU), so the story had more meaning. Also, recall how every Friday, each branch of the Commonwealth Bank and each call centre team got customer feedback on how well they had performed in the previous week, which again kept the momentum going.

The idea is that the voice of the customer, particularly in qualitative comments where customers are actually reporting on their experience, can make an incredible difference. These allow you to "listen" to what customers are saying.

Some of the best ways to capture qualitative comments are:

- customer compliments (complaints should be used carefully as they can be demotivating in the short term),
- mystery shopping feedback,
- qualitative comments on customer feedback forms, and
- stopping customers as they exit the store and asking for a few minutes of feedback.

Let's look at how one company uses the customer voice to drive them forward.

CASE STUDY: Squamish Lil'wat Cultural Centre

WHEN WAS THE last time that you were on your way out of a restaurant and were asked about your experience and invited to give two to three minutes of feedback as to what you liked and didn't like? And I don't mean by the server—because we will *never* say anything bad to them when they ask how the meal was, as it is too socially awkward to tell them about the lifeless hamster you found in the arugula salad.

My answer to that question is never! Incredibly, I have never been stopped by anyone on the way out of a restaurant to ask about my experience and insights. Now, this may say something about the kind of restaurants that I visit, but I find it staggering. Just think of all the amazing data they could collect.

I was a restaurant a few years ago and they gave me the bill with a customer feedback form as well—except this form had already been filled out by a previous customer. They had not taken it out, which told you exactly about what this restaurant *really* thought about customer feedback. Let's just say the feedback by the customer matched the quality of effort the restaurant put into collecting data.

Now think about this. What if you asked five of your customers every day, "What is the one thing you liked the most about your service experience today?" and "What is the one thing you think we could improve on the most?" to make it a better experience for them the next time they used your service? Imagine the useful information you would get from more than 1,000 customers a year.

And that's just what I get organizations to do when I work with them.

The Squamish Lil'wat Cultural Centre is a First Nations museum, café, gift shop, and cultural experience centre. After working with the Squamish Lil'wat Cultural Centre on customer service, I encouraged them to seek more customer feedback as they continuously improve their service.

The Squamish Lil'wat Cultural Centre has been stopping ten visitors on the way out of the door for over a year now, and that practice has provided valuable insights into what they have been doing well and the areas they can improve. As Brady Smith, executive director of the centre, says, "In real time, I implement suggestions that have validity and work out the issues that have a more negative or supportive direction. It's a wonderful tool."

And that's the key: when the customer tells you what you are doing well or poorly, it carries so much more legitimacy than what you think or say about your own performance.

There are so many times where I have given essential customer feedback but it has been ignored. In a recent survey for a hotel chain where I always stay, I suggested that if you stay in a hotel, you should be able to keep the towels that are provided. But no! They still insist on checking my suitcase on my way out and charging me if I take one or two. (I've gotten clever and wear them under my kilt now.)

Despite the critical nature of seeking customer feedback, service firms generally don't ask for open-ended feedback or, if received, don't share it in a meaningful way. But the voice of customers helps you endure when you lose faith. Nothing beats a compliment in motivating employees to persevere in serving customers.

Recap

With no commitments in place, the habits that help you deliver great service consistently will not emerge. You will fall victim to the whirlwind that takes you away from important work. Building commitments—and even streaks—helps you maintain focus on what drives your service success.

The customer voice helps make it all real. Without knowing whether customers are seeing your improved service commitments or, even more basically, what they think about your service, it is hard to stay motivated and accountable. This book is about delivering a better customer experience—what is the value in that if you don't know if it makes any kind of difference to the people who really matter? You should always collect and distribute feedback from your customers—it sounds very simple, but it is so rare to find an organization that commits to this potent practice every single day.

Conclusion

Beyond FAME

OW THAT YOU know the FAME model, the opportunities for you
are wide open.

I feel so close to you now after this journey we have been on
together. Some of you even took me to bed to read—that was awkward
but special, thanks. I hope this journey has been enlightening for you.
Science often is enlightening because it shows us things that we know
to be true but didn't know *why* they were true, or it teaches us things
we didn't think were true at all. Surprise! I hope, at the very minimum,
this book has helped you organize your thoughts as to what your company needs to do next.

Let's recap.

We started by diagnosing how to build a strong brand. By understanding how to build a strong brand and the role that service plays
in building this brand, we can use the FAME model to its fullest
advantage.

F = Build *frameworks* to educate and enable leaders and employees.
I gave you, at a special discount, a framework built on science that can
help you drive your service forward: the 3Rs framework of reliability,
responsiveness, and relationships, which has been adopted by so many
organizations, so you can be confident that it's tried and tested.

A = Create *accountability* so everyone feels responsible for delivering great service. I outlined a program for hardwiring accountability and the tight-loose-tight framework. These tools will enable you to build accountability at the organizational level as well as on the team and individual levels.

M = *Moments* of power: the power of context, expertise, relationships, and problem handling. Together they tell you all you need to know about how to actually *deliver* great service day in and day out.

E = Build *endurance* through the three key disciplines of implementation: coaching, commitments, and customer voice. These enable you to endure when others have lost the will to serve.

But remember, once you have become famous for delivering great service, there is no guarantee that you will hold on to that reputation. Many companies or employees that learn how to deliver a great customer experience become arrogant and insular. They forget the disciplines that made them great and applaud themselves for achieving their service vision, rather than choosing the path where they double down and work harder to be even a little bit better. It is this path I ask you to choose.

Goodbyes

Rory walked toward the backpackers he would be staying with in Queenstown, after saying goodbye to his friends staying on the Kiwi Experience bus.

"Hey, Rory!" shouted Winton. "Did you ever work out the answer to your question?"

Rory turned around and looked puzzled. "What question? Oh, you mean the one about why Kiwi Experience is so successful?"

"That's it! Did you ever work it out? Why we are so famous?"

"Yeah, I think I did . . . No, I know I did," Rory said adamantly. "It's just difficult to express it all. One day I'll definitely put it down on paper," he proclaimed.

"Well, don't forget to mention me when you do," said Winton as he climbed back on the bus to resume his own service journey.

Ten Tips for Moving from Same to FAME

1. *Consistency is king,* not the customer.
2. *Your brand must represent a valuable market offer,* a concept that resonates with your target market and distinguishes you from the competition.
3. Every customer experience is driven first and foremost by being *dependable and keeping your core promises.*
4. By *hardwiring accountability* through the organization and *building a strong service system,* you are more likely to consistently deliver positive experiences.
5. Recognize the power of *understanding the environment* in which your customers and employees reside and manage it to your fullest advantage.
6. Demonstrating *expertise* in every service encounter is the lifeblood of every service business.
7. Building *strong relationships* between customers and between employees and customers creates a strong emotional connection to your brand, one that often separates it from the competition.
8. *Proactively dealing with problems* is a critical moment in service situations.
9. Being successful means always doing whatever you can do to stay ahead of the game. In this respect, it's all about *coaching* your employees so they are always growing.
10. Coaching will help, but *forming commitments* and *sharing the voice of the customer* will ensure you *endure* when others have given up.

Notes

Introduction: Creating Famous Service

1   J. Collins and M.T. Hansen, *Great by Choice: Uncertainty, Chaos and Luck—Why Some Thrive Despite Them All* (New York: Random House, 2011).

2   B. Lang and K.F. Hyde, "Word of Mouth: What We Know and What We Have Yet to Learn," *Journal of Consumer Satisfaction, Dissatisfaction and Complaining Behavior* 26, no. 1 (2013). A fantastic review of the research on satisfaction and WOM.

3   Most of this work has come from the American Customer Satisfaction Index (ASCI) over the last twenty-five years, which shows the impact customer satisfaction makes in many areas such as cash flow, profitability, and share price. What's worthwhile is examining the annual returns of companies listed on the ASCI compared to those in general Standard & Poor's 500. Comparing the two groups of stocks over a seventeen-year period demonstrates that the companies prioritizing customer service are outperforming: the ACSI stock portfolio boasts an almost 660 percent growth through December 31, 2016, whereas the S&P 500 index increases 57 percent. These results are also seen when looking at the comparison of these indexes on an annual return basis. Nearly every year over the past seventeen years, the ACSI stock portfolio has registered a higher yearly performance than the S&P 500.

4   From "ACSI Scores as Financial Indicators," American Customer Satisfaction Index: theacsi.org/national-economic-indicator/financial-indicator. The charts depict the actual performance, before fees and expenses, of an actively

managed long/short portfolio of stocks that are selected based on ACSI score data. The Long/Short Portfolio reflects investment decisions guided by ACSI data used to identify companies with the highest ACSI scores (for long positions) and lowest ACSI scores (for short positions). The Long/Short Portfolio does not reflect the performance of all companies scored by the ACSI.

FAME PART 1: FRAMEWORK

Chapter 1: Building a Strong Service Brand

1   L.L. Berry, "Cultivating Service Brand Equity," *Journal of the Academy of Marketing Science* 28, no. 1 (2000): 128–137.

2   It is also worth noting that, unlike big software firms, Salesforce encouraged salespeople to mix customers, prospects, employees, and partners in all manner of events and community activities. This was a game changer in the early 2000s. Suddenly, a modest administrator was able to present their achievements at Dreamforce, the annual user conference hosted by Salesforce in downtown San Francisco that brought together thought leaders, industry pioneers, and thousands of IT professionals. They created a new kind of net promoter, previously unheard of in the enterprise tech industry.

3   A. Cardenal, "Costco vs. Wal-Mart: Higher Wages Mean Superior Returns for Investors," *Motley Fool* (March 12, 2014): fool.com/investing/general/2014/03/12/costco-vs-wal-mart-higher-wages-mean-superior-retu.aspx.

4   T. Worstall, "Of Course Costco Supports a Higher Minimum Wage: It Already Pays Above It," *Forbes* (March 6, 2013): forbes.com/sites/timworstall/2013/03/06/of-course-costco-supports-a-higher-minimum-wage-it-already-pays-above-it/#7ded501342af.

5   B. Stone, "Costco CEO Craig Jelinek Leads the Cheapest, Happiest Company in the World," *Bloomberg* (June 7, 2013): bloomberg.com/news/articles/2013-06-06/costco-ceo-craig-jelinek-leads-the-cheapest-happiest-company-in-the-world.

6   V. Kumar and A. Pansari, "Measuring the Benefits of Employee Engagement," MIT *Sloan Management Review* 56, no. 4 (2015): 67.

7   By a 200-member countrywide panel at the Toronto International Film Festival.

8   D. Rosenberg, "Study: Amazon.com Is Most Trusted Brand in U.S.," *Cnet* (February 22, 2010): cnet.com/news/study-amazon-com-is-most-trusted-brand-in-u-s/

9   L.L. Berry, "Cultivating Service Brand Equity," 134.

10   T. Soper, "T-Mobile Beats Expectations for Profit and Revenue as It Adds Another 2.1M Customers," *Geekwire* (February 14, 2017): geekwire.com/2017/t-mobile-beats-expectations-profit-earnings-adds-another-1-2m-customers/.

11   J. Sherman, "What Is an 'Uncarrier'? We Ask T-Mobile's Chief Marketing Officer, Mike Sievert," *Digital Trends* (January 23, 2013): digitaltrends.com/mobile/t-mobile-disruptive-mike-sievert/.

12   Press release, "T-Mobile's John Legere Climbs Higher in Employee Ratings of America's Top CEOs" (June 8, 2016): businesswire.com/news/home/20160608006474/en/T-Mobile%E2%80%99s-John-Legere-Climbs-Higher-Employee-Ratings.

13   Press release, "Employee Reviews Land Un-Carrier CEO John Legere in America's Top CEOs Rankings (Again!)" (June 20, 2017): newsroom.t-mobile.com/news-and-blogs/un-carriers-ceo-john-legere-lands-top-in-rankings-again-from-employee-ratings-of-americas-top-ceos.htm.

14   D. Aaker, "5 Lessons from T-Mobile's Game-Changing Strategy," *Prophet* (February 12, 2014): prophet.com/thinking/2014/02/5-lessons-from-t-mobiles-game-changing-strategy/.

15   T-Mobile NASDAQ market summary, sourced from Google Finance on January 22, 2018.

FAME PART 2: ACCOUNTABILITY

1   T. Hsieh, *Delivering Happiness: A Path to Profits, Passion, and Purpose* (New York: Grand Central Publishing, 2010). I've included only some of Zappos's values; they have a few more too.

2   Ibid.

Chapter 2: Creating a Clear, Compelling, and Memorable Service Framework

1   *Oxford English Dictionary* online.

2   E. Almquist, J. Senior, and N. Bloch, "The Elements of Value," *Harvard Business Review* 94, no. 9 (September 2016): 13.

3   A. Parasuraman, V.A. Zeithaml, and L.L. Berry, "SERVQUAL: A Multiple-Item Scale for Measuring Consumer Perceptions of Service Quality," *Journal of Retailing* 64, no. 1 (1988): 12.

4   J.L. Heskett and L.A. Schlesinger, "Putting the Service-Profit Chain to Work," *Harvard Business Review* 72, no. 2 (1994): 164–174.

5   Ibid.

6   The Institute of Customer Service, "State of the Nation Report" (January 2017).

7   A. Taylor, "Top Box: Rediscovering Customer Satisfaction," *Business Horizons* 46, no. 5 (2003): 3–14.

8   Institute of Customer Service, "State of the Nation Report."

9   Nielsen Research, "Doing Better Business," unpublished report (2007).

10   R. Parrish, "The US Customer Experience Index, 2017," Forrester Research (August 1, 2017): forrester.com/report/The+US+Customer+Experience+Index+2017/-/E-RES136424.

11   C. Heath and D. Heath, *The Power of Moments: Why Certain Experiences Have Extraordinary Impact* (New York: Simon and Schuster, 2017).

FAME PART 2: ACCOUNTABILITY
Chapter 3: Designing a Service System

1   C. McChesney, S. Covey, and J. Huling, *The 4 Disciplines of Execution: Achieving Your Wildly Important Goals* (New York: Simon and Schuster, 2012).

2   Ibid.

3   "The Importance of Customer Service at Enterprise Rent-A-Car," Business Case Studies: businesscasestudies.co.uk/enterprise-rent-a-car/the-importance-of-customer-service-at-enterprise-rent-a-car/introduction.html.

4   Press release, Enterprise Rent-A-Car (April 29, 2015).

5   M. Colgate, *8 Moments of Power in Coaching: How to Design and Deliver High-Performance Feedback to All Employees* (Elevate, 2016).

6   D. Pink, *Drive: The Surprising Truth About What Motivates Us* (New York: Penguin, 2011).

7   E.L. Deci and R.M. Ryan, *Intrinsic Motivation and Self-Determination in Human Behavior* (New York: Springer Science & Business Media, 1985).

8   J. Preston, "Richard Branson: Why Business Is about People, People and People," *Virgin Entrepreneur* (August 20, 2014): virgin.com/entrepreneur/richard-branson-why-business-is-about-people-people-and-people.

9   As measured by Roy Morgan, an external and independent market research company that researches tens of thousands of customers on their satisfaction every year; see Roy Morgan Customer Satisfaction data: roymorganonlinestore.com/Awards.aspx?month=5&year=2017&country=01.

FAME PART 3: MOMENTS OF POWER

1   C. Dweck, *Mindset: The New Psychology of Success* (New York: Random House, 2006).

Chapter 4: Power of Context

1   A commonly used example of person-situation interaction is the Stanford Prison experiment where college students participated in a study that simulated a prison setting with some students acting as guards and others as prisoners. The study was terminated when the guards became even more abusive than anticipated. Philip Zimbardo concluded that the study shows evidence of the effect of the situation transcending personality traits. See C. Haney, C. Banks, and P. Zimbardo, "Interpersonal Dynamics in a Simulated Prison," *International Journal of Criminology and Penology* 1 (1973): 69–97; D.T. Kenrick and D.C. Funder, "The Person-Situation Debate: Do Personality Traits Really Exist?," *Personality: Contemporary Theory and Research* (1991).

2   R.K. Greenleaf and L.C. Spears, *Servant Leadership: A Journey into the Nature of Legitimate Power and Greatness* (Mahwah, NJ: Paulist Press, 2002).

3   Ibid.

4   K. Baldacci, "7 Customer Service Lessons from Amazon CEO Jeff Bezos," Salesforce (June 10, 2013): salesforce.com/blog/2013/06/jeff-bezos-lessons.html.

5   C. Dweck, *Mindset*.

6   C.S. Dweck, C.Y. Chiu, and Y.Y. Hong, "Implicit Theories and Their Role in Judgments and Reactions: A Word from Two Perspectives," *Psychological Inquiry* 6, no. 4 (1995): 267–285.

7   C. Dweck, *Mindset*.

8   C.S. Dweck, C.Y. Chiu, and Y.Y. Hong, "Implicit Theories."

9   A. Murphy-Paul, "What Students Do with Feedback," Affirmative Testing Blog (2016).

10 S. Kaufman, *Ungifted: Intelligence Redefined* (New York: Basic Books, 2013).

11 D. Kahneman, *Thinking, Fast and Slow* (New York: Farrar, Straus and Giroux, 2011).

12 Ibid.

13 Ibid.

14 S.B. Shu and A. Gneezy, "Procrastination of Enjoyable Experiences," *Journal of Marketing Research* 47, no. 5 (2010): 933–944.

15   Ibid.

16   K. Keizer, S. Lindenberg, and L. Steg, "The Spreading of Disorder," *Science* 322, no. 5908 (2008): 1681–1685.

17   It's true, look as this research! H. Krasnova, T. Widjaja, P. Buxmann, H. Wenninger, and I. Benbasat, "Research Note—Why Following Friends Can Hurt You: An Exploratory Investigation of the Effects of Envy on Social Networking Sites among College-Age Users," *Information Systems Research* 26, no. 3 (2015): 585–605.

18   Kudos to Yogi Berra, the Baseball Hall of Famer, for this awesome joke!

19   N.J. Goldstein, R.B. Cialdini, and V. Griskevicius, "A Room with a Viewpoint: Using Social Norms to Motivate Environmental Conservation in Hotels," *Journal of Consumer Research* 35, no. 3 (2008): 472–482.

Chapter 5: Power of Expertise

1   G.D. Kang, J. Jame, and K. Alexandris, "Measurement of Internal Service Quality: Application of the SERVQUAL Battery to Internal Service Quality," *Managing Service Quality: An International Journal* 12, no. 5 (2002): 278–291; A. Parasuraman, L.L. Berry, and V.A. Zeithaml, "Refinement and Reassessment of the SERVQUAL Scale," *Journal of Retailing* 67, no. 4 (1991): 420.

2   K.V. Rhoads and R.B. Cialdini, "The Business of Influence: Principles that Lead to Success in Commercial Settings," *The Persuasion Handbook* (Sage, 2002): 513–542.

3   M.C. Foushee, "Dyads at 35,000 Feet: Factors Affecting Group Processes and Aircraft Performance," *American Psychologist* 39 (1984): 885–893.

4   C.R. Harper, C.J. Kidera, and J.F. Cullen, "Study of Simulated Airplane Pilot Incapacitation," *Aerospace Medicine* 42 (1971): 946–948.

5   P.G. Zimbardo, *Lucifer Effect* (Hoboken, NJ: Blackwell Publishing Ltd., 2007).

6   S. Milgram, "Behavioral Study of Obedience," *Journal of Abnormal and Social Psychology* 67 (1963): 371–378.

7   A. Ericsson and R. Pool, *Peak: Secrets from the New Science of Expertise* (Boston, MA: Houghton Mifflin Harcourt, 2016).

8   Ibid.

9   T.W. Leigh, T.E. DeCarlo, D. Allbright, and J. Lollar, "Salesperson Knowledge Distinctions and Sales Performance," *Journal of Personal Selling & Sales Management* 34, no. 2 (2014): 123–140.

10   Ibid.

11 R. Vu, "Achieving Peak Performance: A Conversation with Anders Erics-
    son," *The Psych Report* (May 24, 2016): thepsychreport.com/books/
    achieving-peak-performance-a-conversation-with-anders-ericsson/.

12 A. Ericsson and R. Pool, *Peak.*

13 B. Rettinger, "The Customer as Cocreator of Value," The 2013 Naples Forum
    on Service (2013): naplesforumonservice.it/uploads//files/Rettinger.pdf.

14 B. Moggridge and B. Atkinson, *Designing Interactions* 14 (Cambridge, MA: MIT
    Press, 2007).

15 B. Rettinger, "The Customer as Cocreator of Value."

16 C.K. Prahalad and V. Ramaswamy, "Co-creating Unique Value with Custom-
    ers," *Strategy & Leadership* (2004): 2–7, 31, 121, 133.

17 C. Heath and D. Heath, *Made to Stick: Why Some Ideas Survive and Others Die*
    (New York: Random House, 2007).

18 For a great paper on the use of cognitive control, see E.J. Langer and S. Saegert,
    "Crowding and Cognitive Control," *Journal of Personality and Social Psychology*
    35, no. 3 (1977): 175.

19 For example, for the ninth consecutive year, customers ranked Amazon num-
    ber one in customer satisfaction during the holiday shopping season, according
    to the ForeSee Experience Index: U.S. Retail Edition. For its study, customer
    experience analytics firm ForeSee collected more than 67,600 surveys
    between November 29, 2013, and December 17, 2013, asking consumers to
    rate their satisfaction with the top 100 retailers. ForeSee ranked Amazon high-
    est in overall customer satisfaction in the survey with a score of ninety—the
    highest ever recorded by the firm. In addition, ForeSee found that customers
    ranked Amazon highest in satisfaction with the online experience and also put
    Amazon significantly out front when it came to the mobile shopping experience.
    More information about the survey can be found at ForeSee.com. Also in the
    U.K., Amazon rated highest see L. Davidson, "The Companies with the Best
    Customer Service in the UK," *Telegraph* (January 20, 2016).

18 "Amazon CEO: Focus on Customer Is Key," CNN YouTube channel (September
    25, 2013): youtube.com/watch?v=56GFhr9r36Y.

19 K. Baldacci, "7 Customer Service Lessons from Amazon CEO Jeff Bezos."

20 G. Anders, "Jeff Bezos Gets It," *Forbes* (April 25, 2012): forbes.com/
    global/2012/0507/global-2000-12-amazon-jeff-bezos-gets-it.html.

21 "Gala2017: Jeff Bezos Fireside Chat," Internet Association YouTube channel
    (May 5, 2017): youtube.com/watch?v=LqL3tyCQ1yY.

22 Ibid.

23   K. Baldacci, "7 Customer Service Lessons from Amazon CEO Jeff Bezos."

24   G. Anders, "Jeff Bezos Gets It."

Chapter 6: Power of Relationships

1   Parasuraman, Zeithaml, and Berry, "SERVQUAL: A Multiple-Item Scale for Measuring Consumer Perceptions of Service Quality."

2   J. Girard, "Joe Girard on Becoming the World's Greatest Salesperson," *Harvard Business Review* (July–August 2006).

3   Ibid.

4   Ibid.

5   D.D. Gremler and K.P. Gwinner, "Rapport-Building Behaviors Used by Retail Employees," *Journal of Retailing* 84, no. 3 (2008): 308-324.

6   R.B. Cialdini, *Influence: The Psychology of Persuasion* (New York: HarperCollins, 2007).

7   F. Gouillart and F. Sturdivant, "Spend a Day in the Life of Your Customers," *Harvard Business Review* 72, no. 1 (1994): 116-125.

8   M. Colgate, V. Tong, C. Lee, and J. Farley, "Back from the Brink: Why Customers Stay," *Journal of Service Research* 9, no. 3 (2007): 211-228.

9   D.D. Gremler and K.P. Gwinner, "Rapport-Building Behaviors Used by Retail Employees."

10   R.B. Cialdini, *Influence.*

11   D.D. Gremler and K.P. Gwinner, "Rapport-Building Behaviors Used by Retail Employees."

12   Tourism and Events Queensland, "Hero Experiences Guidebook: Creating Memorable Visitor Experiences" (January 2015): teq.queensland.com/~/media/D8AB2695794B4627A67AB7AA1EBC9863.ashx?la=en-NZ.

13   Early classic studies are D. Byrne and R. Rhamey, "Magnitude of Positive and Negative Reinforcements as a Determinant of Attraction," *Journal of Personality and Social Psychology* 2 (1965): 884-889; and E. Berscheid and E. Walster, *Interpersonal Attraction* (Reading, MA: Addison-Wesley, 1978).

14   R.B. Cialdini, *Influence.*

15   D.D. Gremler and K.P. Gwinner, "Rapport-Building Behaviors Used by Retail Employees."

16   Ibid.

17 Ibid.

18 N. Bendapudi and L.L. Berry, "Customers' Motivations for Maintaining Relationships with Service Providers," *Journal of Retailing* 73 (Spring 1997): 15–37.

19 A. Grant, *Give and Take: A Revolutionary Approach to Success* (New York: Penguin, 2013).

20 Mencius quoted in H. Gensler, *Ethics and the Golden Rule* (New York: Routledge, 2013): 78.

21 R.B. Cialdini, *Influence*.

22 A. Grant, *Give and Take.*

23 Ibid.

24 "Givers Versus Takers: The Surprising Truth about Who Gets Ahead," *Knowledge@Wharton* podcast (April 10, 2013): knowledge.wharton.upenn.edu/article/givers-vs-takers-the-surprising-truth-about-who-gets-ahead/.

25 Ibid.

26 R.B. Cialdini, *Influence*.

27 M. Colgate and P. Danaher, "Implementing a Customer Relationship Strategy: The Asymmetric Impact of Poor Versus Excellent Execution," *Journal of the Academy of Marketing Science* 28, no. 3 (2000): 375–387.

28 Ibid.

Chapter 7: Power of Problem Handling

1 V. Zeithaml, M. Bitner, and D. Gremler, *Services Marketing: Integrating Customer Focus Across the Firm* (McGraw Hill Education: 2006).

2 S. Tax and S. Brown, "Recovering and Learning from Service Failure," *MIT Sloan Management Review* 40, no. 1 (1998): 75.

3 D. Cousins and L. Davison, "Impact of Problem Resolution—A Depth Analysis," ANZMAC Conference (2014).

4 M. McCollough, L.L. Berry, and M. Yadav, "An Empirical Investigation of Customer Satisfaction After Service Failure and Recovery," *Journal of Service Research* 3, no. 2 (2000): 121–137.

5 S. Tax and S. Brown, "Recovering and Learning from Service Failure."

6 Ibid.

7 S. Tax, S. Brown, and M. Chandrashekaran, "Customer Evaluations of Service Complaint Experiences: Implications for Relationship Marketing," *The Journal of Marketing* (1998): 60–76.

8 TARP, "Basic Facts on Customer Complaint Behavior and the Impact of Service on the Bottom Line," ASQ Service Quality Division's Competitive Advantage newsletter (June 1999): 1, 4.

9 "Customer Service Problem Resolution," The Ritz-Carlton Leadership Center (October 22, 2014): ritzcarltonleadershipcenter.com/2014/10/customer-service-problem-resolution/.

10 This story was posted on TripAdvisor: tripadvisor.ca/ShowUserReviews-g3446 7-d85228-r120390922-The_Ritz_Carlton_Naples-Naples_Florida.html.

11 M. Soloman, "Eliminate Customer Service Defects with Ritz-Carlton's Simple System," *Forbes* (January 18, 2015): forbes.com/sites/micahsolomon/2015/01/18/learn-ritz-carltons-simple-system-for-eliminating-customer-service-defects/#835c9426aeea.

12 J. Michelli, *The New Gold Standard: 5 Leadership Principles for Creating a Legendary Customer Experience Courtesy of the Ritz-Carlton Hotel Company* (New York: McGraw Hill Professional, 2008).

13 S. Picton, "Now What Do We Do?" *National Post* (March 27, 2001): 1-2.

14 Ibid.

15 Ibid.

16 S. Tax, M. Colgate, and D. Bowen, "How to Prevent Your Customers from Failing," MIT *Sloan Management Review* 47, no. 3 (2006): 30.

FAME PART 4: ENDURANCE
Chapter 8: Coaching

1 J. Miner, "The Rated Importance, Scientific Validity, and Practical Usefulness of Organizational Behavior Theories," Academy of Management Learning and Education, 2 (2003): 250-268.

2 T. Bauer and B. Erdogan, *An Introduction to Organizational Behavior* (Creative Commons, 2012).

3 G. Latham and E. Locke, "Enhancing the Benefits and Overcoming the Pitfalls of Goal Setting," *Organizational Dynamics* 35 (2006): 332-340.

4 K. Shaw, "Changing the Goal-Setting Process at Microsoft," Academy of Management Executive, 18 (2004): 139-142.

5 G. Latham, "The Motivational Benefits of Goal-Setting," Academy of Management Executive, 18 (2004): 126-129.

6 T. Orlick, *In Pursuit of Excellence* (Champaign, IL: Human Kinetics, 1990).

7   Ibid.

8   B. Peltier, *The Psychology of Executive Coaching: Theory and Application* (Taylor & Francis, 2011).

9   S. Miller, *The Complete Player: The Psychology of Winning Hockey* (Toronto: Stoddart Publishing, 2001).

10   M. Read, "Investigating Organizational Coaching Through an Athletic Coaching Comparison: Determining High Performance Coaching Practices in Organizations," unpublished Ph.D. thesis (Vancouver: University of British Columbia, 2011).

11   See, for example, J. Loehr and T. Schwartz, "The Making of a Corporate Athlete," *Harvard Business Review* (2001): 120-128.

12   P. Wahba, "Apple Extends Lead in U.S. Top 10 Retailers by Sales per Square Foot," *Fortune* (March 13, 2015): fortune.com/2015/03/13/apples-holiday-top-10-retailers-iphone/.

Chapter 9: Building Commitments and Using the Customer's Voice

1   "The Upside of Daily Line-Up," The Ritz-Carlton Leadership Center (December 3, 2014): ritzcarltonleadershipcenter.com/2014/12/upside-daily-line-up/.

2   The survey was conducted with Steve Tax from University of Victoria and Ajith Kumar from Arizona State University.

3   These coaching practices were, for example, goal setting, feedback, skills demonstrations by the coach, and observing employees in their roles.

4   J. Jeffery and J.L. Downs, *Streaking* (unpublished manuscript).

5   Ibid.

Acknowledgements

THERE ARE SOME very special people who made this book possible. Dawn, Peter, and Paul, this book is also for you three amazing people. I love you all very much and treasure your friendship immensely.

Orla, your encouragement and incredible support throughout the whole process and your insightful feedback have made such a difference. Books are almost fun to write when you have a partner as supportive as you. Thank you so much.

Nesha, Callum, and Kian, I'm pretty sure I am not famous for my parenting talents, but I will keep on trying. Thanks for letting me practice on you. I adore you three more than you will ever know.

Amanda Lewis—what can I say? Trena White told me you were amazing, but she was always going to say that, right? Well, you are, and you changed this book (for the better!) in so many ways. Thanks also to Trena, Rony, Annemarie, Crissy, Stephanie, and everyone else who contributed at Page Two.

Erin Beattie, I estimate we sent more than 10,000 WhatsApp messages to get this book done. You gave me so much confidence and incredible assistance every step of the way. I treasure our friendship so much. I hope you are proud of it!

Mechthild "Mecki" Facundo, what can I say? I smile when I think of the experiences, memories, and laughs we have shared. You've been such a support both professionally and personally. You always give me great feedback on what I did well and how I can improve. This book has been no exception. First you wrote the Whistler Experience case study without me needing to ask for it. It just turned up over email one morning, early in the book-writing process! When I needed you most, you cancelled a weekend away to read the final version and make vital changes. I owe you so much. THANK YOU!

Miriam MacDonald, you have been a joy to work with over the last three years and I hope this carries on for many years. You have the brightest future ahead of you. A million thanks for everything you have done for me. I love the case study in the book and I hope you love it too.

Lloyd Daser, you extended the hand of friendship from my day one in Whistler, and you and Kate have become such great friends. I have realized over the last three years what an incredible leader you are and how much your employees look up to you. Every guest who stays in your hotel experiences the "Daser" brand first-hand thanks to the culture you have created. Thank you for your friendship and for the dazzling case study.

Saul Klein, dean of the Peter B. Gustavson School of Business, you are a truly remarkable servant leader. Thanks for believing in me and supporting my books so much.

Dan Pontefract, thank you again. I'm trying to catch up with you, but I never will. Thanks for the bromance!

Other huge contributors were Matt Cameron (thanks for your support for my first book too), Michelle Braden (you have pushed my thinking so much and inspired me to be my best), and Sir Val Litwin.

Thanks also to all those have supported me in this book and my service journey over many years: Jeff Puritt (your kindness towards me has been incredible), Andrew Turner (my personal hero), Barbara Chapman, Jill Snarr, Charmaine Stack, Eddie Isted, Deborah Wickins, Janice Johnson, Jim Dunsdon, Gayle Gorrill, and Sarah Stead.

Finally to all those Derby County fans out there still suffering since my last book—COYR!

About the Author

MARK COLGATE, PH.D., is a professor at the Peter B. Gustavson School of Business, University of Victoria, Canada. His primary research areas are service excellence and coaching. His research has been published in journals such as *Sloan Management Review*, *Journal of the Academy of Marketing Science*, *Journal of Service Research*, and *Journal of Business Research*.

Colgate has taught many courses in service excellence and coaching at undergraduate, postgraduate, and executive levels. He has also taught in China (where he is a regular professor at the China Europe International Business School in Shanghai, the country's leading business school), Australia, New Zealand, and Ireland. Colgate has received two university-wide teaching excellence awards from the University of Auckland, New Zealand, in 2000 and the University of Victoria in 2013.

Colgate was for three years the general manager of customer satisfaction at Commonwealth Bank of Australia, the tenth largest bank in the world. He has also consulted and taught for many companies such as Telus, Whistler Blackcomb, Sony, Kiwi Experience, the British Columbia provincial government, Four Seasons, and Toyota.